Contents

Introduction

PART ONE- MENTAL ILLNESS AND THE RANGE OF ILLNESSES

Chapter 1.
Mental Health and Mental illness Generally   13

Symptoms of mental illness   14
Causes   15
Risk factors   15

Chapter 2.
Severe and Ongoing Mental Illness   19

1. Psychosis   19
The underlying cause of psychosis   20
The diagnosis of psychosis   21
Treatment for psychosis   21
Other complications   22

2. Schitzophrenia   23
What is schitzophrenia?   23
Symptoms   24
Cognitive symptoms   27
Schitzophrenia generally   27
Suicidal tendencies   28
Substance use disorders   29

Treatment of schitzophrenia   30
Anti-psychotic medications   30
Psychosocial treatments   31
Rehabilitation   31
Family education and support   32
Cognitive behavioural therapy   32
Self-help groups   32

3. Bi-Polar Disorder   33
Signs and symptoms of bi-polar disorder   33
Manic episodes   33
Hypomania   34
Depression   34
Signs and symptoms of a mixed episode   35
Different types of bi-polar disorder   36
Length and frequency of episodes   36
What causes bi-polar disorder?   37
Childhood bi-polar disorder   38
Treatment for bi-polar disorder   41
NICE guidance   41
Types of medication   42
Community Mental Health Teams   47
Psychotherapy   47
Care co-ordinators   49
Hospitalisation   50

4. Depression   50
Psychological symptoms of depression   50
Physical symptoms   51
Concentration and memory problems   52
Delusions and hallucinations   52
Suicidal impulses   52

Physical symptoms   53
Sleep problems   53
Mental and physical slowing   53
Loss of appetite   54
Reverse physical symptoms   54
Other physical symptoms   55
Sex   55
Causes of depression   56
Nerve cell releases   56
The role of hormones   57
Juvenile depression   58
Other types of depression   60
Seasonal affective disorder (SAD)   60
Post Traumatic stress disorder (PTSD)   62
Brain damage   63
Depressive personality   64
Anxiety disorder   65
Treating depression   66
Psychological therapy   66
Cognitive behavioural therapy (CBT)   67
Behaviour therapy   68
Psychoanalysis   69
Counselling   70
Mood stabiliser   70
Self-harming and suicide   70

Chapter 3.
Generalised Anxiety Disorders and Personality
                                                     73
Disorders

Generalised anxiety disorder   73
Phobias   74

Panic disorder   75
Agoraphobia   75
Social anxiety disorder (SAD)   76
Post-traumatic stress disorder   77
Obessive compulsive disorder   77
Causes of anxiety disorders   78
Diagnosis   78
Personality disorders   79
Treating a personality disorder   82
Medication   82

Chapter 4.
Mental Health and Older People   83

Causes and risk factors for mental illness in older people   84
Mental illness or aging?   85
The NHS   86

PART TWO-ACCESSING TREATMENT

Chapter 5.
Accessing Treatment-The NHS   89

Mental health services in England   89
Mental health care pathways   91
Accessing treatment   92
Child and adolescent mental health services (CAMHS)   94
Specialist CAMS   95
CAMHS information for parents and carers   96

PART THREE-MENTAL HEALTH AND THE LAW

Chapter 6.
The Mental Capacity Act 2005 (England and Wales)   99
Mental Capacity Acts Scotland and Northern Ireland

How mental capacity is determined	100
Mental capacity and supporting decision making	102
Making best interests decisions for someone	102
Finding alternatives	102
Deprivation of liberty	103
Advance statements and decisions	103
Lasting powers of attorney	104
The Court of Protection	104
Professional's duties under the Act	
Mental Capacity Act-Adults with Incapacity (Scotland) Act 2000	106
The Mental Capacity Act (Northern Ireland) 2016	110

Chapter 7.
The Respective Mental Health Acts England   113
and Wales, Scotland and Northern Ireland

The Human Rights Act 1998	113
The Mental Health Act 1983 as amended	114
Community Treatment Orders (CTO)	116
Detention of voluntary patients	116
Leave of absence	117
Section 12 approved doctors	117

The Mental Health Act Code of Practice   118
The role of hospital managers   119
Nearest relative   120
Powers of the courts to intervene   121
Police powers   122
Guardianship   122
Rights of appeal   124
After leaving hospital   124
The Care Quality Commission   125
Mental Health Law in Scotland   128
Mental health Law in Northern Ireland   131

Resource section-Useful Information

Index

****

8

Introduction to this book

Mental Health is once again at the forefront of discussion and debate in the United Kingdom. One of the main focal points has been children (and young people generally) and mental health.

According to The Mental Health Foundation, mental health problems affect 1 in 10 children and young people. However, 70% of those affected have not had early intervention to prevent the onset of mental illness. This can and does lead to distressing situations, both in a young life and also later in life for the child or young person and their families.

In addition to children and young people, mental illness affects many adults and doesn't seem to be getting any better, with strains of everyday life such as housing shortages, escalating rents and house prices, rising homelessness and levels of personal debt and everthing that flows from these factors having an adverse affect on peoples lives and their mental health. Correspondingly, to make things worse, in the face of the governments austerity drive, mental health services have been squeezed.

Therefore, it is more important than ever that individuals and their families can receive accurate and timely advice to prevernt their personal situation deteriorating. That is why this book has been written.

The book is divided into three parts-the first part highlights the range of different types of mental illnesses that can affect people, from the most severe through to a wide range of other disorders. The second part deals with accessing treatment through the National Health Service and what type of treatment is available, and the third and final part deals with the law and mental health. Because of the fact that the book deals with the United Kingdom as a whole, the law in Scotland and Northern Ireland, as well as the law in England and Wales is covered.

The useful resources section at the back of the book also details the numerous organisations that exist to help people cope with mental illness.

David Wade

****

PART ONE

MENTAL ILLNESS AND THE RANGE OF ILLNESSES

Chapter 1

Mental Health and Mental Illness Generally

Mental Health and Mental Illness Generally

Mental health is defined as a state of well-being in which every individual realizes his or her own potential, can cope with the normal stresses of life, can work productively and fruitfully, and is able to make a contribution to her or his community. (World Health Organisation).

Mental illness refers to a wide range of mental health conditions —disorders that affect mood, thinking and behavior. Examples of mental illness, some of which are covered in more depth in this book, include depression, anxiety disorders, schizophrenia, eating disorders and addictive behaviors.

It is a fact that many people have mental health concerns from time to time. Mental health concerns become a mental illness when ongoing signs and symptoms cause frequent stress and affect your ability to function. This is when you will, inevitably, need help and assistance to restore your equilibrium. and this is what this book is about, what is the law and how can you obtain help?

13

Mental illness can upset lives and cause problems in a persons daily life, such as at school or work or in relationships. In most cases, symptoms can be managed with a combination of medications and talk therapy (psychotherapy).

Symptoms of mental illness

Signs and symptoms of mental illness can vary, depending on the disorder, circumstances and other factors. Mental illness symptoms affect emotions, thoughts and behaviors. Some examples of signs and symptoms include:

- o Feeling sad or down
- o Confused thinking or reduced ability to concentrate
- o Excessive fears or worries, or extreme feelings of guilt
- o Extreme mood changes of highs and lows
- o Significant tiredness, low energy or problems sleeping
- o Detachment from reality (delusions), paranoia or hallucinations
- o Trouble understanding and relating to situations and to people
- o Alcohol or drug abuse
- o Major changes in eating habits
- o Sex drive changes
- o Excessive anger, hostility or violence
- o Suicidal thinking

Causes

Mental illnesses, in general, are thought to be caused by a variety of genetic and environmental factors:

Inherited traits. Mental illness is more common in people whose blood relatives also have a mental illness. Certain genes may increase the risk of developing a mental illness, and a person's life situation may trigger it.

Environmental exposures before birth. Exposure to environmental stressors, inflammatory conditions, toxins, alcohol or drugs while in the womb can sometimes be linked to mental illness.

Brain chemistry. Neurotransmitters are naturally occurring brain chemicals that carry signals to other parts of the brain and body. When the neural networks involving these chemicals are impaired, the function of nerve receptors and nerve systems change, leading to depression

Risk factors

Certain factors may increase the risk of developing mental health problems, including:

o Having a blood relative, such as a parent or sibling, with a mental illness

- o Stressful life situations, such as financial problems, a loved one's death or a divorce
- o An ongoing (chronic) medical condition, such as diabetes
- o Brain damage as a result of a serious injury (traumatic brain injury), such as a violent blow to the head
- o Traumatic experiences, such as military combat or being assaulted
- o Use of alcohol or recreational drugs
- o Being abused or neglected as a child
- o Having few friends or few healthy relationships
- o A previous mental illness

Mental illness is common. About 1 in 5 adults has a mental illness in any given year. Mental illness can begin at any age, from childhood through later adult years, but most begin earlier in life.

Complications

Mental illness is a leading cause of disability. Untreated mental illness can cause severe emotional, behavioral and physical health problems. Complications sometimes linked to mental illness include:

- o Unhappiness and decreased enjoyment of life
- o Family conflicts
- o Relationship difficulties
- o Social isolation

- o Problems with tobacco, alcohol and other drugs
- o Missed work or school, or other problems related to work or school
- o Legal and financial problems
- o Poverty and homelessness
- o Self-harm and harm to others, including suicide or homicide
- o Weakened immune system, so your body has a hard time resisting infections
- o Heart disease and other medical conditions
- o A substance use disorder.

In Chapter 2, we will look more specifically at the nature of severe and ongoing mental illness and look at four main areas:

- o Psychosis
- o Schizophrenia
- o Bi-Polar disorder
- o Depression

In chapter 3 we will look at more generalized disorders., such as anxiety and personality disorders. Following this we will look at the types of treatment available and how to access those treatments, plus the law generally in the UK.

****

Chapter 2

Severe and Ongoing Mental Illnesses

In this chapter, we will look at a range of illnesses classified as severe. As we have seen, there are a very wide range of conditions within the broad spectrum of mental illness. We will examine the most well known and researched: psychosis; schitzophrenia; bi-polar disorder and depression. In chapter 3, we will look at a range of other disorders.

1. Psychosis

The word 'psychosis' derives from the Greek words 'psyche' meaning mind and 'osis' meaning condition. Fundamentally, psychosis is a severe mental health problem that causes people to perceive or interpret things differently from those around them. This could involve Hallucinations or Delusions. There are two main recognised symptoms of psychosis which are:

o   hallucinations – where a person hears, sees and, in some cases, feels, smells or tastes things that aren't there; a common hallucination is hearing voices o delusions – where a person believes things that, when examined rationally, are obviously untrue – for example, thinking your friends are planning to kill you

The combination of hallucinations and delusional thinking can lead to a psychotic episode which will often severely disrupt a person's perception, thinking, emotion, and behaviour.

The underlying cause of psychosis

Psychosis is, basically, triggered by other conditions. It's sometimes possible to identify the cause of psychosis as a specific mental health condition, such as:

o schizophrenia – a condition that causes a range of psychological symptoms, including hallucinations and delusions

o bipolar disorder – a mental health condition that affects mood; a person with bipolar disorder can have episodes of depression (lows) and mania (highs)

o severe depression – some people with depression also have symptoms of psychosis when they're very depressed

Psychosis can also be triggered by other problems such as traumatic experiences, stress, or physical conditions, such as drug misuse or alcohol misuse. How often a psychotic episode occurs and how long it lasts can depend on the underlying cause. For example, schizophrenia can be long term, but most people can make a good recovery and about a quarter only have a single psychotic episode.

The Diagnosis of psychosis

A person's GP will usually get involved immediatly if a person is experiencing psychotic episodes. It's important that psychosis is treated as soon as possible as treatment in the early stages usually has better long-term outcomes. A GP will look at a patients symptoms and may ask: whether the patient is taking any medication; whether they have been taking illegal substances; how their general mood mood has been – for example, whether they have been depressed. In addition they will ask about day to day functions and whether there is a history of mental health. They will try to ascertain whether the person is hallucinating, i.e. whether they have heard voices and also about delusions – such as whether they feel people are controlling them. A GP should then refer a patient to a mental health specialist for further assessment and treatment.

Treatment for psychosis

Mainstream Treatment for psychosis will involve using a combination of: antipsychotic medication – which can help relieve the symptoms of psychosis and psychological therapies –

i.e one-to-one talking therapy. Cognitive therapy has proved successful in helping people with schizophrenia; in appropriate cases, family therapy has been shown to reduce the need for hospital treatment in people with psychosis. In addition social support – support with social needs, such as education, employment, or accommodation is vital.

Most people with psychosis who get better with medication need to continue taking it for at least a year. Some people need to take medication long-term to prevent symptoms recurring. However, if a person's psychotic episodes are too severe, they will need to be admitted to a psychiatric hospital. People with psychosis often have a lack of insight. They're unaware that they're thinking and acting strangely. Because of their lack of insight, it's often down to the friends, relatives, or carers of a person affected by psychosis to seek help for them.

Other complications arising as a result of psychosis
People with a history of psychosis are much more likely to have drug or alcohol misuse problems, or both. These substances can provide short-term symptom relief, although they will inevitably usually make symptoms worse in the long term.

A sad fact is that people with psychosis also have a higher than average risk of suicide. It's estimated 20% of people with psychosis will attempt to commit suicide at some point in their life, and 1 in 25 people with psychosis will kill themselves. Side effects can also occur if someone is taking antipsychotics on a long-term basis. Weight gain is a common side effect.

2. Schitzophrenia

What is schizophrenia?

Schizophrenia is a chronic and severe disorder that affects how a person thinks, feels, and acts. Although schizophrenia is not as common as other mental disorders, it can be very disabling. Approximately 7 or 8 individuals out of 1,000 will have schizophrenia in their lifetime. People with the disorder may hear voices or see things that aren't there. They may believe other people are reading their minds, controlling their thoughts, or plotting to harm them. This can be scary and upsetting to people with the illness and make them withdrawn or extremely agitated. It can also be scary and upsetting to the people around them.

People with schizophrenia may sometimes talk about strange or unusual ideas, which can make it difficult to carry on a conversation. They may sit for hours without moving or talking. Sometimes people with schizophrenia seem perfectly fine until they talk about what they are really thinking.

Families and society are also impacted by schizophrenia. Many people with schizophrenia have difficulty holding a job or caring for themselves, so they may rely on others for help. Stigmatizing attitudes and beliefs about schizophrenia are common and sometimes interfere with people's willingness to talk about and get treatment for the disorder. People with schizophrenia may cope with symptoms throughout their lives, but treatment helps many to recover and pursue their life goals.

The symptoms of schizophrenia

The symptoms of schizophrenia fall into three broad categories: positive, negative, and cognitive symptoms.

Positive Symptoms

Positive symptoms are psychotic behaviors not generally seen in healthy people. People with positive symptoms may "lose touch" with some aspects of reality. For some people, these symptoms come and go. For others, they stay stable over time. Sometimes they are severe, and at other times hardly noticeable. The severity of positive symptoms may depend on whether the individual is receiving treatment. Positive symptoms include the following:

Hallucinations are sensory experiences that occur in the absence of a stimulus. These can occur in any of the five senses (vision, hearing, smell, taste, or touch). "Voices" (auditory hallucinations) are the most common type of hallucination in schizophrenia. Many people with the disorder hear voices. The voices can either be internal, seeming to come from within one's own mind, or they can be external, in which case they can seem to be as real as another person speaking. The voices may talk to the person about his or her behavior, command the person to do things, or warn the person of danger. Sometimes the voices talk to each other, and sometimes people with schizophrenia talk to the voices that they hear. People with schizophrenia may hear voices for a long time before family and friends notice the problem. Other types of hallucinations include seeing people or objects that are not there, smelling odors that no one else detects, and feeling things like invisible fingers touching their bodies when no one is near.

Delusions are strongly held false beliefs that are not consistent with the person's culture. Delusions persist even when there is evidence that the beliefs are not true or logical. People with schizophrenia can have delusions that seem bizarre.

Sometimes they believe they are someone else, such as a famous historical figure. They may have paranoid delusions and believe that others are trying to harm them, such as by cheating, harassing, poisoning, spying on, or plotting against them or the people they care about. These beliefs are called "persecutory delusions."

Thought disorders are unusual or dysfunctional ways of thinking. One form is called "disorganized thinking." This is when a person has trouble organizing his or her thoughts or connecting them logically. He or she may talk in a garbled way that is hard to understand. This is often called "word salad." Another form is called "thought blocking." This is when a person stops speaking abruptly in the middle of a thought. When asked why he or she stopped talking, the person may say that it felt as if the thought had been taken out of his or her head. Finally, a person with a thought disorder might make up meaningless words, or "neologisms."

Movement disorders may appear as agitated body movements. A person with a movement disorder may repeat certain motions over and over. In the other extreme, a person may become catatonic. Catatonia is a state in which a person does not move and does not respond to others. Catatonia is rare today, but it was more common when treatment for schizophrenia was not available.

Negative Symptoms

Negative symptoms are associated with disruptions to normal emotions and behaviors. These symptoms are harder to recognize as part of the disorder and can be mistaken for depression or other conditions.

These symptoms include the following:

- o "Flat affect" (reduced expression of emotions via facial expression or voice tone) o Reduced feelings of pleasure in everyday life

o Difficulty beginning and sustaining activities

o Reduced speaking

People with negative symptoms may need help with everyday tasks. They may neglect basic personal hygiene. This may make them seem lazy or unwilling to help themselves, but the problems are symptoms caused by schizophrenia.

Cognitive Symptoms

For some people, the cognitive symptoms of schizophrenia are subtle, but for others, they are more severe and patients may notice changes in their memory or other aspects of thinking. Similar to negative symptoms, cognitive symptoms may be difficult to recognize as part of the disorder. Often, they are detected only when specific tests are performed. Poor cognition is related to worse employment and social outcomes and can be distressing to individuals with schizophrenia.

Schitzophrenia generally

Schizophrenia affects slightly more males than females. It occurs in all ethnic groups around the world. Symptoms such as hallucinations and delusions usually start between ages 16 and 30. Males tend to experience symptoms a little earlier than females. Most commonly, schizophrenia occurs in late adolescence and early adulthood. It is uncommon to be diagnosed with schizophrenia after age 45. Schizophrenia rarely occurs in children, but awareness of childhood-onset schizophrenia is increasing.

It can be difficult to diagnose schizophrenia in teens. This is because the first signs can include a change of friends, a drop in grades, sleep problems, and irritability—behaviors that are common among teens. A combination of factors can predict schizophrenia in up to 80 percent of youth who are at high risk of developing the illness. These factors include isolating oneself and withdrawing from others, an increase in unusual thoughts and suspicions, and a family history of psychosis. This pre-psychotic stage of the disorder is called the "prodromal" period.

Suicidal tendencies

Suicidal thoughts and behaviors are very common among people with schizophrenia. People with schizophrenia die earlier than people without a mental illness, partly because of the increased suicide risk.

It is hard to predict which people with schizophrenia are more likely to die by suicide, but actively treating any co-existing depressive symptoms and substance abuse may reduce suicide risk. People who take their antipsychotic medications as prescribed are less likely to attempt suicide than those who do not.

Substance use disorders

Substance use disorders occur when frequent use of alcohol and/or drugs interferes with a person's health, family, work, school, and social life. Substance use is the most common co-occurring disorder in people with schizophrenia. Substance use disorders can make treatment for schizophrenia less effective, and individuals are also less likely to engage in treatment for their mental illness if they are abusing substances. It is commonly believed that people with schizophrenia who also abuse substances are trying to "self-medicate" their symptoms, but there is little evidence that people begin to abuse substances in response to symptoms or that abusing substances reduces symptoms.

Cannabis (marijuana) is frequently abused by people with schizophrenia, which can worsen health outcomes. Heavy cannabis use is associated with more severe and earlier onset of schizophrenia symptoms, but research has not yet definitively determined whether cannabis directly causes schizophrenia.

Drug abuse can increase rates of other medical illnesses (such as hepatitis, heart disease, and infectious disease) as well as suicide, trauma, and homelessness in people with schizophrenia.

It is generally understood that schizophrenia and substance use disorders have strong genetic risk factors. While substance use disorder and a family history of psychosis have individually been identified as risk factors for schizophrenia, it is less well understood if and how these factors are related.

When people have both schizophrenia and a substance abuse disorder, their best chance for recovery is a treatment program that integrates the schizophrenia and substance abuse treatment.

The treatment of schitzophrenia

Because the causes of schizophrenia are still unknown, treatments focus on eliminating the symptoms of the disease. Treatments include antipsychotic medications and various psychosocial treatments.

Antipsychotic Medications

Antipsychotic medications have been available since the mid-1950s. The older types are called conventional or typical antipsychotics. In the 1990s, new antipsychotic medications were developed. These new medications are called second-generation or *atypical* antipsychotics. Some people have side effects when they start taking medications. Most side effects go away after a few days. Others are persistent but can often be managed successfully.

Atypical antipsychotic medications can cause major weight gain and changes in a person's metabolism. This may increase a person's risk of getting diabetes and high cholesterol.

Antipsychotic medications are usually taken daily in pill or liquid form. Some antipsychotics are injections that are given once or twice a month. Symptoms of schizophrenia, such as feeling agitated and having hallucinations, usually improve within days after starting antipsychotic treatment. Symptoms like delusions usually improve within a few weeks. After about 6 weeks, many people will experience improvement in their symptoms. Some people will continue to have some symptoms, but usually medication helps to keep the symptoms from getting very intense.

Psychosocial Treatments

Psychosocial treatments can help people with schizophrenia who are already stabilized. Psychosocial treatments help individuals deal with the everyday challenges of their illness, such as difficulty with communication, work, and forming and keeping relationships. Learning and using coping skills to address these problems helps people with schizophrenia to pursue their life goals, such as attending school or work. Individuals who participate in regular psychosocial treatment are less likely to have relapses or be hospitalized.

Rehabilitation

Rehabilitation emphasizes social and vocational training to help people with schizophrenia participate fully in their communities. Because schizophrenia usually develops during the critical career-development years (ages 18 to 35), the career and life trajectories for individuals with schizophrenia are usually interrupted and they need to learn new skills to get their work life back on track. Rehabilitation programs can include employment services, money management counseling, and skills training to maintain positive relationships.

Family Education and Support

Family education and support teaches relatives or interested individuals about schizophrenia and its treatment and strengthens their capacity to aid in their loved one's recovery.

Cognitive Behavioral Therapy

The CBT therapist teaches people with schizophrenia how to test the reality of their thoughts and perceptions, how to "not listen" to their voices, and how to manage their symptoms overall. CBT can help reduce the severity of symptoms and reduce the risk of relapse. CBT can be delivered individually or in groups.

Self-Help Groups

In self-help groups for people with schizophrenia, group members support and comfort each other and share information on helpful coping strategies and services. Professional therapists usually are not involved. People in self-help groups know that others are facing the same problems, which can help everyone feel less isolated and more connected.

3. Bi-Polar Disorder

Signs and symptoms of bi-polar disorder

There are four types of mood episode in bipolar disorder: mania, hypomania, depression and mixed episodes.

Manic episodes

In the manic phase of bipolar disorder, feelings of heightened energy, creativity, and euphoria are common. People experiencing a manic episode often talk very fast, sleep very little and are hyperactive Such a person may feel that they are all-powerful, invincible or destined for greatness. To summarise, symptoms might include:

- o A feeling of euphoria
- o Feelings of restlessness
- o Extreme irritability
- o Talking very fast
- o Racing thoughts
- o lack of concentration
- o Lots of energy
- o A reduced need for sleep
- o A sense of own importance
- o Poor judgement
- o Excessive and inappropriate spending
- o Increased sexual drive
- o Risky behaviour

- o Misuse of drugs or alcohol
- o Aggressive behaviour

While mania might feel good in the first instance, it has a tendency to spiral out of control. The aggressive side of mania can be a particular problem, picking fights, lashing out and so on.

Hypomania

Hypomania is a less severe form of mania. people in a hypomanic state feel euphoric, energetic and productive, but they are able to carry on with their day-to-day lives and they never lose touch with reality. To others, it may seem that people with hypomania are in an unusually good mood. However, hypomania can result in bad decisions that can harm relationships with others and also harm careers and reputations. In addition, hypomania can also escalate to a full-blown mania.

Depression

In the past, bipolar depression was seen as general depression. Doctors couldn't differentiate. However, a growing body of research suggests that there is a significant difference between the two, especially when it comes to recommended treatments. Whereas doctors tend to prescribe anti-depressants in many cases, these will not always help those with bipolar disorder. In fact, it has been proved that they can make the condition worse, triggering mania.

Despite many similarities, certain symptoms are more common in bipolar depression than in regular depression. For example, bipolar depression is more likely to involve irritability, guilt, unpredictable mood swings and restlessness. People with bipolar depression also tend to move and speak slowly, sleep a lot and gain weight. In addition, they are more likely to develop psychotic depression-a condition where a person loses contact with reality and also to experience major problems with social functioning, which can affect work.

Common symptoms of bipolar depression include:

o Feeling hopeless, sad or empty

o Irritability

o Inability to experience pleasure

o Fatigue or loss of energy

o Physical or mental sluggishness

o Appetite or weight changes

o Sleep problems

o Concentration and memory problems

o Feelings of worthlessness or guilt

o Thoughts of death or suicide

Signs and symptoms of a mixed episode

A mixed episode of bipolar disorder, as its name suggests, is where a person will exhibit symptoms of both mania, hypomania and depression. Common signs of a mixed episode include depression combined with agitation, irritability, anxiety, distractibility and racing thoughts. This combination of moods makes for a very high risk of suicide.

Different types of bipolar disorder

Bipolar disorder is further categorized as:

- o Bipolar 1 disorder, which is mania or mixed episode. This is the classic manic-depressive form of the illness, characterized by at least one manic or mixed episode. Usually, but not in all cases, bipolar 1 will involve at least one episode of depression.
- o Bipolar 2 disorder (hypomania and depression). In bipolar 2 disorder the person doesn't experience full blown manic episodes. Instead the illness involves a mixture of hypomania and severe depression.
- o Cyclothymia (hypermania and mild depression). Cyclothymia is a milder form of bipolar disorder. It consists of cyclical mood swings. However, the symptoms are less severe than full-blown mania or depression.

Length and frequency of episodes

A person may have very few bipolar disorder episodes, with years of stability in between each episode. However, they may also experience many more. Episodes can vary in length and frequency from weeks to months, with varying lengths of time in between.

Mania usually starts suddenly and lasts between two weeks and four to five months. Depression often lasts longer, on average around six months, but can last longer, but usually less than a year. Although a person may cope very well in between episodes, they may experience low-level symptoms in these relatively 'stable' periods which can impact on daily life.

What causes bipolar disorder?

Like a lot of other conditions, for example, Parkinson's, very little is known about the sources of bipolar disorder. However, it does run in families, which suggests a genetic link. On the other hand, there may not be a family link and the origin may lie elsewhere. This is one of the problems with diagnosing the causes of bipolar disorder. Unless the link is obvious then the origins remain obscure. The disorder is diagnosed in a roughly equal number of men or women. It usually starts in the 20's and 30's, although it can also start as a teenager.

The fact that symptoms can be controlled by medication, especially lithium and anticonvulsants suggests that there may be problems with the functions of the nerves in the brain. This is supported by research. Disturbances in the endocrine system (controlling hormones) may also be involved.

Most research suggests that a stressful environment, social factors, or physical illness may trigger the condition. Although stress is unlikely to cause bipolar disorder, it seems to be a significant trigger. A person may find that the start of bipolar episodes can be linked to a period of great stress, such as childbirth, a relationship breakdown, money problems or a career change. Sleep disturbance can be an important contributor.

Childhood distress

Some experts believe that a person may develop bipolar disorder if they experienced severe emotional damage in early life, such as physical, sexual or emotional abuse. Grief, loss trauma and neglect can be contributory factors-they can shock the developing mind and produce unbearable stress.

General problems in life

It is also very possible that bipolar disorder can be a reaction to overwhelming problems in day-to-day life. Mania can be a way of escaping unbearable depression. For example, if a person appears to have very over-inflated sense of one's own self-importance and place in society, they may be compensating for a severe lack of self-confidence and lack of self-esteem.

Childhood bi-polar disorder

Childhood bipolar disorder, also known as pediatric bipolar disorder, is a form of bipolar disorder that occurs, as its name suggests, in children. While its existence is still a matter of some academic debate and disagreement, there is a growing body of evidence that suggests that bipolar disorder can exist in children.

Unlike most adults who have bipolar disorder, however, children who have pediatric bipolar disorder are characterized by abrupt mood swings, periods of hyperactivity followed by lethargy, intense temper tantrums, frustration and defiant behavior. This rapid and severe cycling between moods may produce a type of chronic irritability with few clear periods of peace between episodes.

Because the current diagnostic manual of mental disorders doesn't recognize childhood bipolar disorder, there is no official symptom criteria. However, researchers have used criteria similar to that of adult bipolar disorder, requiring a child or teen to meet at least four or more of the following:

- an expansive or irritable mood
- extreme sadness or lack of interest in play
- rapidly changing moods lasting a few hours to a few days
- explosive, lengthy, and often destructive rages
- separation anxiety
- defiance of authority
- hyperactivity, agitation, and distractibility
- sleeping little or, alternatively, sleeping too much

- ○ bed-wetting and night terrors
- ○ strong and frequent cravings, often for carbohydrates and sweets
- ○ excessive involvement in multiple projects and activities
- ○ impaired judgment, impulsivity, racing thoughts, and pressure to keep talking
- ○ dare-devil behaviors (such as jumping out of moving cars
- ○ inappropriate or precocious sexual behavior
- ○ grandiose belief in own abilities that defy the laws of logic (ability to fly, for example)

Keep in mind that many of these behaviors, in and of themselves, are not indicative of a possible disorder and are characteristic of normal childhood development. For instance, separation anxiety, by itself, is a normal fear of being separated from one or both of the parents (for instance, attending the first day of school or if the parents want to go out for a night).

Childhood bipolar disorder is characterized by many of these symptoms, taken together, and marked by rapid mood swings and hyperactivity. These symptoms must also cause significant distress in the child or teen, occur in more than just one setting (e.g. at school and at home), and last for at least 2 weeks.

Treatment for Bipolar Disorder-Initial Diagnosis and Medication

If a GP thinks that a person has bi-polar disorder, they may refer them to a psychiatrist. A psychiatrist or GP should explain all of the options to the sufferer and their views should be taken into account before treatment starts.

NICE Guidance

The National Institute for Health and Care Excellence (NICE) has guidelines for the treatment of bipolar disorder. They suggest that a person should be offered structured psychological treatment while they are relatively stable but may be experiencing mild to moderate symptoms. Usually, the psychological treatment would be given in addition to medication and a person should be offered at least 16 sessions.

The treatment should cover:

o Education about the illness-including information about the importance of regular daily routine and sleep, and about any medication that they have agreed to take

o How to monitor their moods, detect early warning signs and strategies to prevent symptoms from developing into full-blown episodes

o General coping strategies.

Virtually everyone who has been diagnosed with bipolar disorder will receive medication of one sort or another. Although drugs cannot cure bipolar disorder they help to manage the symptoms. Drugs used include lithium, anticonvulsants and anti-psychotics.

Types of medication

Lithium

Lithium is a mood stabilizer and is the most common form of medication for those with bipolar disorder. It is the most effective medication for treating mania. It can also help depression. However, it is not really effective for mixed episodes. Lithium will take between one to two weeks to take effect.

Lithium is a naturally occurring element, the lightest of the metals and comes as two different salts: Lithium carbonate (Camcolit, Liskonum, Priadel) and Lithium Citrate (Li-Liquid, Priadel).

It is very important that lithium is taken at the right level and regular blood tests are essential. It is also very important to drink plenty of fluids every day and alcohol should be taken in moderation as well as coffee and strong tea.

Anticonvulsant drugs

Some other drugs are commonly used as mood stabilizers, Sodium valproate and Carbamazepine plus Lamotrigine.

Although both were initially used for the management of epilepsy, they have been found to offer benefits to bi-polar patients. Sodium valproate, (common names: Epilim, Divalproex, Depakote) has been found to be effective in patients who suffer predominantly from depression. Common side effects can be: Nausea, vomiting, weight gain, tremors, drowsiness, hair loss.

Carbamazepine, (common name: Tegretolks), works less well in such cases. Common side effects: Dry mouth, nausea, diarrhoea, dizziness, headaches, problems with walking, tiredness and rashes.

Lamotrigine has anti-depressant effects and is licensed for depressive episodes in bipolar disorder. Like lithium anticonvulsants also have to be monitored for excess levels, although not as tightly as lithium. They can also present some risk during pregnancy

Anti-depressants

Anti-depressants are not the most effective drugs for those with bipolar disorder. There are a number of different types of anti-depressants, but the two most commonly prescribed are the Trcyclic anti-depressants (TCA's) and the serotonin reuptake inhibitors (SSRI's). The first type has been in use a long time now and the second type for about ten years. Both are effective and both take between two weeks and a month to relieve

43

depression. However, both types of drugs have differing side effects.

In bi-polar disorder, these drugs may be used during depressive episodes. However, as mentioned the side effects can present a danger. There is a risk, in some people that anti-depressants can trigger an episode of mania. People with bi-polar should probably be on a mood stabilizer if taking anti-depressants and, as a rule, not take them for more than six months.

The TCA's

Examples of these drugs include Amitriptyline (Lentizol/Elavil), dothiepin/dosulepin (prothiaden) and lofepramine (Gamanil).

Side effects of these drugs: they have a wide variety of side effects, which are often more pronounced during the early stages of taking the drug. Common side effects include tiredness and excessive sedation, dry mouth, constipation and difficulty in urinating. After the first few weeks, these side effects should decrease.

The SSRI's

Examples include fluoexetine (Prozac), paroxetine (Seroxat, paxil) citalopram (Cipramil, Cipram) and sertraline (Lustral, Zoloft). There are also some newer, related antidepressants, including venlafaxine (Efexor) and nefazodone (Dutonin). All of these drugs have weird and wonderful names, but some are more well know than others, such as Prozac, which has had a lot of bad press.

Side effects: these drugs are said to have fewer side effects than the trycyclics and are, supposedly, safer in the event of an overdose. However, they can have a number of varied side effects, including upset stomach, headaches, agitation and rashes. Like most side effects they subside over time.

One other class of anti-depressant that is sometimes prescribed is the monoamine oxidase (MAO) inhibitors. These were the first antidepressants, but most of them cannot be mixed with certain foods, such as cheeses and yeast products. For this reason, they are rarely prescribed. However, a new type of MAO inhibitor, moclobemide (Manerix) does not require dietary restriction.

Antipsychotic drugs (Neuroleptics)

Some anti-psychotic drugs are licensed for the treatment of mania. Their main use is in the treatment of psychosis and they have been shown to reduce or eliminate many of the symptoms of psychosis, such as delusions and hallucinations. In bi-polar disorder, they are used during acute manic episodes to calm the patient, slow racing thoughts and help with sleep. Some of the newer anti-psychotics have mood stabilizing properties. There are a number of different neuroleptics, such as: chlorpromazine

(Largactil, Thorazine) haloperidol (Haldol) and trifluoperazine (Stelazine). Newer neuroleptics include risperidone (Risperdal) amisulpride (Solian) and olanzapine (Zyprexa) which are said to have fewer side effects and be easier to take.

Side-effects

All of the above drugs are associated with potentially serious side effects and should be used at the lowest effective dose for the shortest time. Side effects include sedation (sleepiness), dry mouth, weight gain, constipation and sensitivity to sunlight. A common class of side effects, the so-called extrapyramidal or parkinsonian side effects, include stiffness and restlessness.

Anti-parkinsonian drugs

These drugs are sometimes given with neuroleptics to relieve side effects. They are not prescribed initially, but only as a treatment for extrapyramidal side-effects if they develop. Anti-parkinsonian drugs include procyclidine (Kemadrin) benzatropine, (Cogentin) and benzhexol/trihexphenidl (Broflex). Side effects of these drugs can include dry mouth, stomach upsets, blurred vision and dizziness.

Minor tranquillisers

These medications, also known as *benzodiazepines* have been used for years to cure anxiety and insomnia. Valium is one of the better known but there are a number of other drugs within the same type. They provide quick relief from anxiety and sleeplessness and, if taken correctly, have fewer side effects. The main problem with these drugs is the risk of dependency. Common benzodiazepines include diazepam (Valium) lorazapam (Ativan) and clonazepam (Rivotril).

Community mental health teams

If a person has been referred to psychiatric services in England or Wales, by a GP, they have a right to get their needs assessed and a care plan developed for them within the Care Programme Approach (CPA). The plan should include a thorough assessment of social and health care needs. They should be allocated a care-coordinator who is in charge of their care and ongoing reviews. They are entitled to say what their needs are and also to have an advocate present. An advocate is someone who can speak for them if necessary. Often, community care assessments are made by Community Mental Health Teams. Their aim is to help people live independently. They can also help with practical issues, such as sorting out welfare benefits if appropriate and also other services, such as day-centres, or drop in centres. They can also arrange for a Community Psychiatric Nurse (CPN) to visit a home.

Psychotherapy

Psychotherapy is another vital part of bipolar disorder treatment. Several types of therapy may be helpful. These include:

Cognitive behavioral therapy. This is a common form of individual therapy for bipolar disorder. The focus of cognitive behavioral therapy is identifying unhealthy, negative beliefs and behaviors and replacing them with healthy, positive ones. It can help identify what triggers your bipolar episodes. A person acncan also learn effective strategies to manage stress and to cope with upsetting situations.

Psychoeducation. Counselling to help people learn about bipolar disorder (psychoeducation) can help them and their loved ones understand bipolar disorder. Knowing what's going on can help them get the best support and treatment, and help them and their loved ones recognize warning signs of mood swings.

Family therapy. Family therapy involves seeing a psychologist or other mental health provider along with other family members. Family therapy can help identify and reduce stress within a family. It can help a family learn how to communicate better, solve problems and resolve conflicts.

Group therapy. Group therapy provides a forum to communicate with and learn from others in a similar situation. It may also help build better relationship skills.

Other therapies. Other therapies that have been studied with some evidence of success include early identification and therapy for worsening symptoms (prodrome detection) and therapy to identify and resolve problems with daily routines and interpersonal relationships (interpersonal and social rhythm therapy).

Psychodynamic therapists

Psychodynamic theraprists have traditionally viewed psychological and psychiatric problems as originating in a person's childhood and development. Courses of therapy are usually longer than with cognitive behavioural therapy, and the therapy may focus less on specific problems and more on personal relationships. Psychodynamic therapists can be dotcors, psychologists or members of other professions. In addition to being funded by the NHS, it is possible to seek therapy privately.

Care co-ordinators

Over the last few decades, as medications have become more effective, it has become very unusual indeed for people with serious mental illness to spend very long periods in hospital. More and more effeort has gone into helping people to live in the in the community. This approach has had varying degrees of success.

In the UK, one key part of this approach, called the care programme approach, calls for certain people to be monitored out in the community by a care co-ordinator who is usually either a nurse or a social worker. The care co-ordinator is supposed to meet with the patient regularly, offer advice and support and make sure that he or she is staying well and receiving guidance on taking medication and receiving all other services to which they may be entitled.

If a person is in receipt of benefits, or having financial problems, the care co-ordinator can offer practical support. The care co-ordinator is also supposed to convene regular meetings of all involved with the patients care, but this will only happen if the illness is very severe.

Hospitalization

In some cases, usually for short periods, people with bipolar disorder benefit from hospitalization. Getting psychiatric treatment at a hospital can help keep stay safe and calm and stabilize moods, whether they are having a manic episode or a deep depression.

4. Depression

Depression can show itself in two distinct ways, psychologically and physically. Some of the psychological symptoms may be a result of the physical symptoms and vice versa. Sometimes the physical symptoms aren't even noticed because the psychological symptoms are so bad.

Psychological symptoms of depression

- o Constantly anxious
- o Emotionally numb
- o Low moods
- o Persistent feeling of sadness

o Feeling empty

o A sense of loss or dread

o A low mood worse in the morning (Diurnal Variation)

o Nothing seems to bring any pleasure (Anhedonia)

o Low mood may seem worse in the evenings

o The odd good day, outnumbered by the bad

o Crying more often from slight or even no upset

o Depressive thinking

o Concentration and memory problems

o Delusions

o Hallucinations

o Suicidal impulses

Physical symptoms of depression

o Difficulty with sleeping (getting to sleep/waking too early/sleeping too much)

o Mental and physical slowing

o Increase or decrease in appetite

o Increase or decrease in weight

o Problems with libido

o Tiredness and lethargy, aches and pains

o Constipation

o Problems with the menstrual cycle

Concentration and memory problems.

When a sufferer is in a state of depression, it can be hard to focus on anything within their world. Anyone who needs to remember facts needs to be able to concentrate, so if a person suffers with depression, their memory can also be poor. They become indecisive or inattentive, don't listen well or get muddled by instructions and confused. Again, it becomes a vicious circle. (An elderly sufferer of depression with this symptom may have it misdiagnosed as the start of dementia.)

Delusions and hallucinations

These severe symptoms usually only occur if a person is severely depressed. Their mind begins to lose touch with reality. It can play tricks. Or, at least, it seems to. A patient may fear they are going mad. Hallucinations and delusions are rare in depression.

The hallucinations may manifest themselves as false images, sounds or voices, whereas delusions manifest themselves as false beliefs.

Suicidal impulses

When hit by a severe bout of depression, all of a person's life may appear to be awful, without hope for the future and full of past mistakes. The present may seem pointless and incredibly painful to be in. A person may find themselves wondering if life is worth living?

Physical symptoms of depression

Some depressive cases may present themselves with physical symptoms only and make them harder to spot. A sufferer may believe that they have something physical wrong with them. However, doctors are trained to spot these cases, too. Some of these physical symptoms that may manifest themselves, are explained below.

Sleep problems

These kinds of problems are common in depression and vary in their form. A sufferer may present with the inability to get to sleep. Or they may present with the fact that they sleep too much.

A patient may feel tired and sleepy all day, yawning constantly or they may find that when they do sleep, their sleep is disturbed. They toss and turn and constantly wake to check the clock. Others may wake extremely early or have a combination of these symptoms.

Mental and physical slowing

Sometimes, a patient may say to their doctor that they feel they are constantly moving through treacle. Their bodies feel like they are seizing up from the inside and struggling to carry out everyday tasks. They're tired, their muscles ache, despite taking painkillers. Everything for them is such an effort to do. They feel like they're living in a slow-motion world. They might even talk slowly, it's such an effort. Movements are slow (psychomotor retardation), their mouth is dry constantly, they get constipated or their periods have stopped/become irregular. They may worry that physically, they have something seriously wrong with them.

Loss of appetite

A depressed person may lose some weight through loss of appetite and without eating a nutritional, balanced diet, may leave themselves open to infection or ill health. Interest in food is at an all-time low and when they do eat, the food tastes bland and uninteresting. If their mouth is dry, they may have difficulty chewing and swallowing the food. They may not feel like bothering with meals at all. Or a sufferer may simply never feel hungry. Then as their bodies run on no fuel at all, they become tired and lethargic. It can all become a vicious circle that seems impossible to sort.

Reverse physical symptoms

Of all of the these symptoms above, a few depressive sufferers may find that they are affected by the exact reverse of the problems. They may overeat, sleep too much, gain large amounts of weight or be hyperactive. In any of these cases, it is imperative to be seen by a GP.

Other physical symptoms

Depression can cause plenty of other physical symptoms in a sufferer such as generalised aches and pains, sore joints, feeling pressure in the head, the face, the spine, chest or stomach.

Sex

Perhaps one of the most physical symptoms of depression is an effect on libido, the sexual drive. Many depressed patients feel that they have no interest in sex with their partner. This can be caused not only by the actual physical disinterest, but also can be affected if the sufferer feels generally numb about the world. If they're agitated, they may experience an inability to relax or in the case of a man, get and maintain an erection. Women feel they cannot be aroused, or that intercourse is painful and their bodies are unable to respond in the normal way. Some sufferers may feel that they are just totally unable to say why they don't want to be intimate. Lack of libido can cause great problems and issues in a relationship, so an abrupt change in libido would certainly be cause to consult a doctor.

Cause of these symptoms

So what causes depression? And all these symptoms, whether physical or mental? It's certainly a complicated cocktail of chemicals and hormones, balance and measure. And to understand how this might affect any of us, we must have a basic understanding of how our brains work.

The human brain, whether male or female, is made of billions of nerve cells. Hundreds, if not thousands of these nerve cells are utilised to carry out a single action, whether it's the eyes blinking, or simply just having a thought.

For these nerve cells to work properly and efficiently they need to be able to communicate with each other and to do this, they release a special chemical called a neurotransmitter, from the ends of themselves into spaces between the cells. These spaces are called synapses.

Nerve cell releases

In the brain, there are actually different types of neurotransmitters, most importantly, noradrenaline, serotonin and dopamine. You may have heard of any of these. Noradrenaline (norepinephrine) is a hormone closely related to adrenaline, with similar actions. It is secreted by the medulla (the inner area) of the adrenal gland. Its many jobs are the constriction of small blood vessels, leading to an increase in blood pressure, increased blood flow through the coronary arteries and a slowing of the heart rate, increase in the rate and depth of breathing and relaxation of the smooth muscle in the intestinal wall. Serotonin (5-hydroxytryptamine) is vastly distributed in the central nervous system, the intestinal wall and in the blood platelets. Serotonin is used in the treatment of migraines and its levels in the brain are a great influence on mood. Drugs that have serotonin as its heart, are utilised widely in the treatment of depression in the form of anti-depressants. Dopamine acts on certain dopamine receptors and also on adrenergic receptors throughout the body especially in the extrapyramidal system of the brain and in the heart's arteries. Dopamine also stimulates the release of noradrenaline from nerve endings.]

These three neurotransmitters will be in short supply if person is suffering with depression. The synapses are low in these important chemicals, leading to a breakdown in communication and faulty connections of messages, directly causing depressive symptoms. When a doctor prescribes anti-depressants, they are increasing the levels of these chemicals and the neurotransmitters to assist in normal brain communication.

The role of hormones

Hormones are equally to blame in causing the symptoms of depression. The hormone adrenaline, in high quantities, can cause anxiety. Cortisol is our bodies reaction to stress.

Cortisol is a steroid hormone and when we are stressed, we release amounts of it into our body from the adrenal cortex, causing alterations in our immune reactions, our kidney function and effects the levels of fats and sugars in our blood supply. The control of the release of cortisol is in the pituitary gland of the brain. If a person is healthy, a large amount of cortisol is released into the body in the morning, allowing it to diminish throughout the rest of the day. But if a person is depressed, a large amount of cortisol is released all day long and as you can see from the above information, this one hormone alone could cause significant changes in our body and mood.

Juvenile depression

It is unfortunate that in this day and age that young children actually suffer with depression, and many parents/adults do not believe that children are capable of suffering with it.

The term 'juvenile' is restricted to those that are seventeen years of age, or below and sadly, juvenile depression is a lot more common than most people would like to believe, affecting about two in every hundred children before they hit puberty and averaging around nine in every one hundred adolescents. In the teenage years, girls, more than boys, seem to be affected more and there is a distinct lack of enjoyment in activities that they once found pleasurable. They lose their appetite, their sleep patterns are poor and inconsistent. Some gain weight, rather than lose it, as they seek comfort in food high in calories and show an abnormal amount of concern for their own health and wellbeing. Teachers may notice that a child's school performance may drop. There are even some teenagers who think about self-harming, or even harbour thoughts on suicide.

Boys may find it tough, in that they might have been raised not to show their inner feelings and emotions so that they feel they cannot admit to being upset or sad, or feeling the need to cry and therefore show their turmoil instead in extreme acts of irritability or acting bored/being destructive/self-harming.

The difficulties in teenagers suffering with depression and being diagnosed, is that most people will automatically assume that the teenager is simply being hormonal, and therefore 'typical' of being a teenager.

Some youngsters, like adults, are not able to cope with the stresses and strains of their everyday life and depression results. They may be unable to cope with:

o   Starting a new school
o   Making friends
o   Being bullied/teased on a day to day basis
o   Unable to cope with school work
o   Problems in the home, such as marriage break up, having a single parent, having a parent addicted to a substance, abuse, poverty, being fostered, adopted, etc
o   Hormonal changes as they approach puberty
o   Problems with menstruation
o   Long-term illness
o   Social issues

- o Exam pressures
- o A death of a parent or family member

Depression in young people is often found to occur alongside other mental health disorders, such as anxiety, being constantly disruptive or abusing illegal substances, or even with the physical disorders such as diabetes.

Other types of depression

As as been seen, there are many different types and causes of depression and not all of them have the same symptoms. A patient may have clinical depression and then suffer with an episode of post traumatic stress disorder. Another may have post-natal depression, but also suffer with seasonal affective disorder.

Seasonal affective disorder (SAD)

SAD is a disorder which occurs in a patient according to the season of the year, typically as winter approaches. The patient's mood is drastically affected. Depression sets in and they feel sluggish, not only in body but also in the mind. Thought processes may be slow. They may be forgetful or irritated by small upsets. A lot of sufferers with SAD note a preponderance of needing lots of extra sleep, and general lethargy and malaise become quite a problem. Other sufferers may note that their appetite does not so much increase (in that they feel hungry) but just that tend to eat more, especially carbohydrates and sugar rich foods, such as biscuits, cakes, potatoes. Low mood seems to be worse in the afternoons and evenings, but their symptoms start to resolve with the coming of spring time. (SAD may account for the higher suicide rates that occur during the winter months.) Women seem to be affected by SAD more than men are, but what is SAD?

Some doctors believe that mood is related to light, as light is instrumental in the release of melatonin, a hormone created in the pineal gland. (Melatonin is a hormone that is released in the body when it is dark and not when the light is bright. Melatonin receptors in the brain react to the hormone and help the body to recognise when it is night-time and when it is day time. Melatonin is derived from serotonin which helps work to regulate and organise a person's sleep patterns.)

If a person is diagnosed with SAD then they may find that they benefit from using Light Therapy. A lot of sufferers have found this type of therapy most effective and though they do not lose all of their depressive symptoms, they do feel a lot better in coping with their day and have more energy and 'get-up-and-go'.

Treatment consists of sitting in front of what is called a 'light box'. This is a box that contains full spectrum light and to feel any benefit, the person has to sit in front of it for a few hours each day. This full spectrum light is a doppelganger of natural sunlight, the lack of which appears to be the cause of SAD. Some sufferers state that they get the most benefit from this treatment if they use it in the mornings and results are usually seen after a week.

Post-traumatic stress disorder (PTSD)

Post traumatic stress disorder is a difficult disorder to diagnose as the effects may not be seen immediately after an event. PTSD is a reactive depression initially, which may then become endogenous. This condition occurs specifically after someone has been exposed to an extreme of stress such as a violent crime, being raped, witnessing a terrorist attack or being involved in one, serving during a war, etc.

The initial trauma of such a condition, may be experienced as flashbacks. The sufferer sees the event happening again, over and over in explicit detail, with sound, smell and sensory overdrive. The flashbacks can occur during the day, causing panic attacks, hyperventilation and nausea, or at night time when the patient is asleep, resulting in nightmares and broken sleep, sweating and feverishness.

The patient may stop eating, may stop venturing out and withdraw from society, family and friends. They may become extremely irritable and snappy or even turn to a substance such as alcohol to cope with getting through the hours. At its worst extremes, a sufferer may even harbour thoughts of suicide, especially if they suffer feelings of 'survivor guilt'.

A GP will be able to diagnose the condition and it is one that will settle with time, but a patient usually requires external help with the support of skilled and registered counsellors, psychologists or psychiatrists, that may utilise Cognitive Behavioural Therapy (CBT) or Behaviour Therapy (BT).

Brain damage

Damage can occur to the brain through various ways, especially as a result of trauma/accident or disease and after damage has occurred, symptoms similar to depression may occur. (Hearing a diagnosis of brain damage can also be such a shock, it can be quite similar to the effect of PTSD.)

For example, Alzheimer's Disease (a form of dementia, characterised by short-term memory loss, deterioration in 'normal' behaviour and intellect) can be hidden by a previous diagnosis of depression, or even misdiagnosed as depression, especially in elderly patients.

Coping with a long-term illness or a person knowing they have a condition that is causing significant or insignificant brain damage can also cause the onset of depression.

Patients with a long-term illness or those that have suffered brain damage as the result of an accident, may be offered counselling to help cope with their condition in an attempt to help prevent the onset of depression. However, some patients may be so angry or in such denial that they refuse such offers. In these cases, it may be up to the family and friends of the patient to get the names and numbers of any helpful associations so that if the patient changes their mind at a later date and feels the need to just talk about how they feel, then they have somewhere and someone to whom they can go. (

Depressive personality

Having a depressing/pessimistic personality does not preclude someone from actually developing depression.

Depressive personality in itself in not an illness. It is a character trait. That person would be of the 'wine glass always being half-empty' kind of mindset. Normal everyday activities always have a down side. For example, any possible car journeys will be marred by their constant gloomy observations. Other drivers' bad habits, the amount of traffic, the fact that when they get to wherever they are going the place will no doubt be overrun and busy. They'll get upset at traffic lights and cyclists and generally everything is usually everyone else's fault or you hear 'this sort of thing always happens to me!'

Yet depressive personalities can also develop any kind of depression (my father has a pessimistic personality and also SAD) and it would take an extremely talented member of their family to notice if that person also suffered with depression.

Anxiety disorder

If a person has an anxiety disorder, it does not mean that they will automatically get a depressive disorder, but it can predispose them to it. Anxiety disorders may develop from phobias, psychosomatic illness (believeing there to be something wrong with their body, when there isn't), obsessions and compulsions or a dysfunction in the body. Suffering with extreme nerves, not being confident or having good self-esteem can also create an anxiety disorder.

It is when these anxieties become so much part of the sufferers' life that it overtakes everything else that depression can set in. The event causing the anxiety controls so much of the sufferers' life that they feel they cannot do everyday things can lead to that depression and then the symptoms of depression also make everything a whole lot worse. It very much becomes a vicious cycle and can quite quickly become such an issue, the sufferer does not know what actually came first and what the root of their problem is! Anxiety disorders can benefit greatly from cognitive behavioural therapy and general counselling and many people benefit from these types of treatment for their anxiety and depression.

Treating depression

Professionals have various ways of treating depression according to the age of the patient and what kind of depression they are suffering from. If the depression is severe, a doctor may strongly recommend a person take the tablets he/she has prescribed and refer you to a psychiatrist. A GP may also want them to come back after a few weeks for a check-up to see how they are getting on with their tablets and whether the dosage or variant of medication needs alteration.

If tablets do not work and they are still severely depressed they may be offered hospital treatment, possibly admitted if the situation is extremely bad and they are suicidal. However, different doctors may proceed differently, depending upon the case.

Psychological therapy

Psychology deals with the study of behaviour and all of its related mental processes. It mainly concerns itself with rational and irrational thoughts, memories, learning, personality, emotions and their relationship to behaviour.

There are different schools of psychological thought, such as those that believe in Freud, or Jung. But there are also those that believe in behaviourism and cognition as being more important and leading the way, and certainly, cognitive behavioural therapy, at the moment, seems to be 'all the rage'. yet having said this, it does not mean that all psychologists belong to one school of thought or another. There are many professionals who take a little from each of the beliefs and apply it to their individual clients according to the problems being presented, as different therapies benefit different conditions and different clients.

Psychological therapy will best suit those patients who do not want to take any medication for their depression. Also, there are some clients who really benefit from getting deep into their mental and emotional past to find the root causes for their depression, because in the present, they just cannot see a reason for their condition. Therapy however, takes time and commitment from the patient to keep going. This isn't just a one-off session they will have. Each therapy session usually consists of one hour, once a week, but can be for longer or even more frequently depending upon how they are in themselves or how severe their problem is.

Cognitive behavioural therapy (CBT)

Cognitive Behavioural Therapy is a type of psychotherapy which is based on the belief that psychological problems are there because of a patients' faulty way of thinking about their world. The cognitive behavioural therapist listens to, assists and helps that patient identify these faulty ways of thinking and shows them a different way of thinking to avoid the initial problem.

CBT seems to work well in mild, moderate, or even severe, depressive cases, and remember, it can also be used in conjunction with medication, or without.

Behaviour therapy

Behaviour therapy is completely different to cognitive therapy in that cognitive therapy tackles how a person thinks, whereas behaviour therapy tackles what they do. It does not focus on why they feel so depressed, but rather acts on making them act less depressed. For example, they would be encouraged and educated in how to look after themselves better. A superior eating programme and lifestyle is suggested, ensuring sleep patterns are regular and making sure they get a good amount of exercise, the theory being that if they look after their self better, behave better, it stops them slumping into the depression as they are actively taking care of themselves.

This kind of therapy may benefit those with less severe cases of depression and those people who always feel better doing something about problems, rather than talking about them.

Remember, not everyone is comfortable talking about their problems or how they think or what happened in their past. They may do eventually, but to start off with, behavioural therapy could help because the patient is physically involved in tackling their problem.

Psychoanalysis

This is a long-term treatment, developing over many sessions and many topics, not just the depression, but also other events in peoples life.

Psychoanalysts believe that any problems we have in our current lives, and the problems they are causing, have their origins in our pasts. That these past problems were something we did not deal with at the time and so now they are 'rearing their heads' in our current lives. These past problems may have been ignored or denied. Or we may have even tried to forget them, believing that if we don't think about them, giving them their power, then they will go away, only to have these problems haunt us in the present. Festering away in the backs of our minds and causing us upset and possibly the depression that sent us to them in the first place.

Psychoanalysis is said to work by the way it assists these past, darker feelings in coming to the forefront of our minds, allowing us to see them for what they are. Analyse them. Talk about them. Deal with them. In effect, lessening the effect the past pain used to have and weakening its effect, allowing you, as a whole person, to move on. It allows repressed thoughts to the surface and encourages 'free-thinking'.

Counselling

Counsellors do exactly as they are described. They counsel. They help people to solve a problem, maybe suggesting another way they could tackle certain issues and encourage them to think about things and life. They will not give specific advice but will assist in helping to sort problems.

Mood stabilisers

Some doctors may prefer to try patients out on a mood stabiliser, more commonly given to epileptic patients, if they are unsuitable to take lithium. These anticonvulsant drugs are used in people who have seizures but do not show themselves as having convulsions. They are called carbamazepine (trade name Tegretol. Can actually be used with lithium), lamotrigine (trade name Lamictal), phenytoin (trade name Epanutin), sodium valproate (trade name Epilim. To be used with caution in pregnancy), topiramate, gabapentin, levetiracetam, oxcarbazepine and vigabatrin.

Self-harming and suicide

Unfortunately, some people suffering with depression, will feel the need to self-harm or harbour thoughts of committing suicide.

The two are not inexorably linked. If a person self-harms, it does not necessarily mean they will think of, or try to commit suicide. And if they feel suicidal, it does not mean that they will have previously self-harmed. Only sometimes a few people will harm themselves before going on to think or try to kill themselves.

Self-harming can take many forms. Sufferers may poison themselves with a deliberate overdose of some harmful substance (but not enough to be fatal) to suffer the consequences. They may hit themselves where bruises will not be seen or where an explanation can be readily created. (eg, "Oh, I caught my leg on the corner of the table.") Others may cut themselves with blades or broken glass, they might attempt to burn themselves with lit cigarettes or hold their hands over a lighted match. Some will pull at their hair, often removing huge amounts or pick at their skin, peeling it away until it bleeds. Others may scratch themselves or pinch themselves, whilst others may attempt more brutal forms such as self-strangulation until the feeling of passing out comes close, before they stop.

Self-harming is not a realistic way to deal with stress and upset or depression. It just appears that way to the sufferer at the time. So what they need are new ways of thinking and to be given new coping mechanisms, along with any medication prescribed by their doctor.

Suicide

This is obviously a very serious part of depression however it is important to state that just because someone feels depressed, it does not mean they will get suicidal.

However, there will be a few people affected by suicide, or suicidal thoughts, when they are depressed and it is more common in certain groups than in others, though the reason why is unknown.

The majority of people who attempt to commit suicide, thankfully do not die and it is also quite rare to find a child under the age of 14 who wants or has tried to kill themselves. However, older teenagers do try to commit suicide and out of 100,000 15-19 year olds, there are 13 suicides. Whether all of these were intentional in causing death, or whether some were only a cry for help that went wrong, we don't know. Young males are more prone to committing suicide in this age group and it tends to occur with those males who have had a previous history of mental illness, have used drugs, abused alcohol, have made previous failed attempts on their lives or they are a relative of a suicide victim.

****

Chapter 3

Generalised Anxiety Disorders and Personality Disorders

In chapter 3, we covered four main disorders which are considered severe. However, anxiety disorder and personality diorders which manifest themselves in numerous ways can also cause distress and effectively stop people from interacting with other people and society as a whole. Firstly, whilst recognising that there are numerous anxiety disorders, we will look at Generalised Anxiety Disorders which cover a number of conditions that give rise to anxiety.

Generalized Anxiety Disorder

Generalized anxiety disorder (GAD) is a common, chronic disorder characterized by long-lasting anxiety that is not focused on any one object or situation. Those suffering from generalized anxiety disorder experience non-specific persistent fear and worry, and become overly concerned with everyday matters. Generalized anxiety disorder is characterized by chronic excessive worry accompanied by three or more of the following symptoms: restlessness, fatigue, concentration problems, irritability, muscle tension, and sleep disturbance. Generalized anxiety disorder is the most common anxiety disorder to affect older adults. Anxiety can be a symptom of a medical or substance abuse problem. A diagnosis of GAD is made when a person has been excessively worried about an everyday problem for six months or more. A person may find that they have problems making daily decisions and remembering commitments as a result of lack of concentration/preoccupation with worry. Appearance looks strained, with increased sweating from the hands, feet, and they may be tearful, which can suggest depression.

In children GAD may be associated with headaches, restlessness, abdominal pain, and heart palpitations. Typically it begins around 8 to 9 years of age.

Phobias

The single largest category of anxiety disorders is that of phobic disorders, which includes all cases in which fear and anxiety are triggered by a specific stimulus or situation. Between 5% and 12% of the population worldwide suffer from phobic disorders. Sufferers typically anticipate terrifying consequences from encountering the object of their fear, which can be anything from an animal to a location to a bodily fluid to a particular situation. Sufferers understand that their fear is not proportional to the actual potential danger but still are overwhelmed by it.

Panic disorder

With panic disorder, a person has brief attacks of intense terror and apprehension, often marked by trembling, shaking, confusion, dizziness, nausea, and/or difficulty. These panic attacks, defined as fear or discomfort that abruptly arises and peaks in less than ten minutes, can last for several hours. Attacks can be triggered by stress, fear, or even exercise; the specific cause is not always apparent.

In addition to recurrent unexpected panic attacks, a diagnosis of panic disorder requires that said attacks have chronic consequences: either worry over the attacks' potential implications, persistent fear of future attacks, or significant changes in behavior related to the attacks. As such, those suffering from panic disorder experience symptoms even outside specific panic episodes. Often, normal changes in heartbeat are noticed by a panic sufferer, leading them to think something is wrong with their heart or they are about to have another panic attack. In some cases, a heightened awareness of body functioning occurs during panic attacks, wherein any perceived physiological change is interpreted as a possible life-threatening illness

Agoraphobia

Agoraphobia is the specific anxiety about being in a place or situation where escape is difficult or embarrassing or where help may be unavailable. Agoraphobia is strongly linked with panic disorder and is often precipitated by the fear of having a panic attack. A common manifestation involves needing to be in constant view of a door or other escape route. In addition to the fears themselves, the term agoraphobia is often used to refer to avoidance behaviors that sufferers often develop. For example, following a panic attack while driving, someone suffering from agoraphobia may develop anxiety over driving and will therefore avoid driving. These avoidance behaviors can often have serious consequences and often reinforce the fear they are caused by.

Social anxiety disorder

Social anxiety disorder (SAD; also known as social phobia) describes an intense fear and avoidance of negative public scrutiny, public embarrassment, humiliation, or social interaction. This fear can be specific to particular social situations (such as public speaking) or, more typically, is experienced in most (or all) social interactions.

Social anxiety often manifests specific physical symptoms, including blushing, sweating, and difficulty speaking. As with all phobic disorders, those suffering from social anxiety often will attempt to avoid the source of their anxiety; in the case of social anxiety this is particularly problematic, and in severe cases can lead to complete social isolation.

Post-traumatic stress disorder (PTSD)

We referred to PTSD in the last chapter. Post-traumatic stress can result from an extreme situation, such as combat, natural disaster, rape, hostage situations, child abuse, bullying, or even a serious accident. It can also result from long-term (chronic) exposure to severe stress, for example soldiers who endure individual battles but cannot cope with continuous combat. Common symptoms include hypervigilance, flashbacks, avoidant behaviors, anxiety, anger and depression. There are a number of treatments that form the basis of the care plan for those suffering with PTSD. Such treatments include cognitive behavioral therapy (CBT), psychotherapy and support from family and friends.

Obsessive–compulsive disorder

Obsessive–compulsive disorder (OCD) is a condition where the person has obsessions (distressing, persistent, and intrusive thoughts or images) and/or compulsions (urges to repeatedly perform specific acts or rituals), that are not caused by drugs or physical order, and which cause distress or social dysfunction. The compulsive rituals are personal rules followed to relieve the anxiety. OCD affects roughly 1-2% of adults (somewhat more women than men), and under 3% of children and adolescents. A person with OCD knows that the symptoms are unreasonable and struggles against both the thoughts and the behavior. Their symptoms could be related to external events they fear (such as their home burning down because they forget to turn off the stove) or worry that they will behave inappropriately.

Causes

Drugs

Anxiety and depression can be caused by alcohol abuse, which in most cases improves with prolonged abstinence. Even moderate, sustained alcohol use may increase anxiety levels in some individuals and dependence can worsen or cause anxiety and panic attacks.

Stress

Anxiety disorders can arise in response to life stresses such as financial worries or chronic physical illness. Anxiety among adolescents and young adults is common due to the stresses of social interaction, evaluation, and body image. Anxiety is also common among older people who have dementia.

Genetics

GAD runs in families and is six times more common in the children of someone with the condition.

Diagnosis

Anxiety disorders are often severe chronic conditions, which can be present from an early age or begin suddenly after a triggering event. They are prone to flare up at times of high stress and are frequently accompanied by physiological symptoms such as headache, sweating, muscle spasms, tachycardia, palpitations, and hypertension, which in some cases lead to fatigue or exhaustion.

Anxiety disorders often occur along with other mental disorders, in particular depression, which may occur in as many as 60% of people with anxiety disorders. The fact that there is considerable overlap between symptoms of anxiety and depression, and that the same environmental triggers can provoke symptoms in either condition, may help to explain this high rate of comorbidity.

Sexual dysfunction often accompanies anxiety disorders, although it is difficult to determine whether anxiety causes the sexual dysfunction or whether they arise from a common cause. The most common manifestations in individuals with anxiety disorder are avoidance of intercourse, premature ejaculation or erectile dysfunction among men and pain during intercourse among women. Sexual dysfunction is particularly common among people affected by panic disorder (who may fear that a panic attack will occur during sexual arousal) and posttraumatic stress disorder.

Personality Disorders

Paranoid personality disorder

If a person has been diagnosed with paranoid personality disorder they may feel very suspicious of others without there being a reason to be. This suspicion can make them feel other people are lying to or exploiting them. This can make it difficult to trust others, even friends.

Schizoid personality disorder

With schizoid personality disorder, a person may have few social relationships and will prefer to be alone. They might actually be very shy, but other people may think them quite cold and distant.

Schizotypal personality disorder

Schizotypal personality disorder is where a person has problems with social and interpersonal relationships. They may have strange thoughts, feel paranoid and see or hear things that aren't there. They may also lack emotion..

Antisocial personality disorder (ASPD)

If a person is diagnosed with antisocial personality disorder (ASPD), they may be impulsive or reckless without thinking of the impact on others. They may get easily frustrated, aggressive and be prone to violence. Others may see this as acting selfishly and without guilt.

Borderline personality disorder (BPD)

If a person has borderline personality disorder (BPD), they may have strong emotions, mood swings and feel they can't cope with life easily. They may feel anxious and distressed a lot of the time and have problems with self-image and thei identity. They may self-harm or use drugs and alcohol to cope with these feelings. This can affect the relationships they have with other people.

Histrionic personality disorder

If a person has a diagnosis of histrionic personality disorder, they may find that they like being the centre of attention and feel anxious about being ignored. This can cause them to be lively and over-dramatic.

Narcissistic personality disorder

Narcissistic personality disorder can mean a person has a sense of inflated self-importance. They may have fantasies about unlimited success and want attention and admiration. They may feel they are more entitled to things than other people, and act selfishly to gain such success. They may do this because inside, they don't feel significant or important.

Dependent personality disorder

If a person has dependent personality disorder, they may allow other people to take responsibility for parts of their life. They may lack self-confidence or be unable to do normal things alone and may find that they put their own needs second to the needs of others, and feel hopeless or fear being alone.

Avoidant personality disorder

If a person has avoidant personality disorder they may have a fear of being judged negatively. This can cause them to feel uncomfortable in social situations. They may be sensitive to criticism, worry a lot and have low self-esteem.

Treating a personality disorder

Treatment for most personality disorders usually involves a course of psychological therapy. There are a range of therapies-psychodynamic (reflective) psychotherapy, Cognitive behavioural therapy and Interpersonal therapy. There are also Therapeutic communities.

Therapeutic communities (TCs) are a form of group therapy, in which the experience of having a personality disorder is explored in depth. TCs are an intensive form of therapy.

Medications

There is no single medication for personality disorders. Medication can be prescribed, for example, if a symptom of a personality disorder is depression. Medications are very much dependant on any subsequent conditions arising.

****

Chapter 4

Mental Health and Older People

Key facts-The World Health Organisation: Globally, the population is ageing rapidly. Between 2015 and 2050, the proportion of the world's population over 60 years will nearly double, from 12% to 22%. Mental health and emotional well-being are as important in older age as at any other time of life. Approximately 15% of adults aged 60 and over suffer from a mental disorder.

Older adults, those aged 60 or above, make important contributions to society as family members, volunteers and as active participants in the workforce. While most have good mental health, many older adults are at risk of developing mental disorders, neurological disorders or substance use problems as well as other health conditions such as diabetes, hearing loss, and Osteoarthritis. Furthermore, as people age, they are more likely to experience several conditions at the same time. **(WHO)**

The most common mental health issue among the elderly is severe cognitive impairment or dementia, particularly caused by Alzheimer's disease. Depression and mood disorders are also fairly widespread among older adults, and disturbingly, they often go undiagnosed and untreated.

Often going along with depression in many individuals, anxiety is also one of the more prevalent mental health problems among the elderly. Anxiety disorders encompass a range of issues, from obsessive-compulsive disorder (including hoarding syndrome) to phobias to post-traumatic stress disorder (PTSD).

Causes and Risk Factors for Mental Illness in older people

One of the ongoing problem with diagnosis and treatment of mental illness in older people is the fact that older adults are more likely to report physical symptoms than psychiatric complaints. However, even the normal physical and emotional stresses that go along with aging can be risk factors for mental illnesses like anxiety and depression. Mental illness in the elderly can include:

- o Physical disability
- o Long-term illness (e.g., heart disease or cancer)
- o Dementia-causing illness (e.g. Alzheimer's disease)
- o Physical illnesses that can affect thought, memory, and emotion (e.g. thyroid or adrenal disease)
- o Change of environment, like moving into assisted living
- o Illness or loss of a loved one
- o Medication interactions

o Alcohol or substance abuse

o Poor diet or malnutrition

As people age, it's natural for some changes to occur. Regular forgetfulness is one thing, however persistent memory loss or cognitive impairment is another thing and potentially serious.

The same goes for extreme anxiety or long-term depression. Relatives and friends should keep an eye out for the following warning signs, which could indicate a mental health concern:

o Sad or depressed mood lasting longer than two weeks

o Social withdrawal; loss of interest in things that used to be enjoyable

o Unexplained fatigue, energy loss, or sleep changes

o Confusion, disorientation, problems with concentration or decision-making

o Increase or decrease in appetite; changes in weight

o Memory loss, especially recent or short-term memory problems

o Feelings of worthlessness, inappropriate guilt, helplessness; thoughts of suicide

o Physical problems that can't otherwise be explained: aches, constipation, etc.

o Changes in appearance or dress, or problems maintaining the home or yard o Trouble handling finances or working with numbers

The NHS

The NHS has a well developed service for identifying and treating mental illness in old age. It is one of the many important range of services they provide. In the next chapter we will look at accessing treatment generally through the NHS.

****

PART TWO

ACCESSING TREATMENT

Chapter 5

Accessing Treatment - The NHS

As we have seen in chapters 3 and 4, there are a wide range of mental disorders, some more prevalent than others. The maintenance of mental health and preventing mental disorder is of great importance to the indiviual and society. However, there are persistent calls for more resources to be allocated to the field of mental health.

In the following two chapters we will be looking at how an individual or those around them can access treatment for their condition and also the law and the powers given to authorities to treat individuals through the Mental Health Acts. The infomation deals with England. Respective NHS services in the rest of the UK will be similar.

Mental health services in England

Mental health services in England deal with a wide range of issues, such as:

o   depression

o   anxiety disorders, including panic attacks and phobias

o   psychosis conditions

o   obsessive compulsive disorders

o   eating disorders

o   trauma-related conditions, such as post-traumatic stress disorder

o   perinatal mental health conditions, including postpartum psychosis

o   children's mental health conditions

o   drugs and alcohol services

o   ADHD and autism spectrum conditions

o   dementia

o   mental health conditions related to living with long-term conditions

This means mental health services have to be able to cater for people from all walks of life and with very different needs.

Mental health services in England are generally run in the following categories:

o   adult services

o   child and adolescent services

o   forensic services

o   learning disability services

o   older adult's services

o   substance misuse services

How these services are organised in each local area may differ. This means some may not cover all mental health conditions, or only deal with people of a certain age. For example, some areas offer services for young people between the ages of 16 and 25 to help with transitions from children to adult services. A GP, local mental health care provider or relevant clinical commissioning group (CCG) has information about what services are available in their area.

Mental health care pathways

How people access services will depend on individual circumstances, such as their age, the specific problem, or how urgently care is required. This means that in addition to the different services, there are also different care pathways.

Again, depending on how services are arranged in a local area, a person may find specific teams that only deal with one particular care pathway – for example, an eating disorders team. But there are also teams that address a variety of disorders in one common pathway, such as community care for anxiety and depression. Some pathways will work across teams and settings.

The website NHS Emotional Wellbeing has detailed information about the different care pathways available under each mental health service specialist area.

Accessing treatment

All mental health services are free on the NHS, as with all services. And as with other condirions, a person will, in most cases , need to be referred by their GP, although there are limited services where they can self-refer such as those that treat drug and alcohol problems.

If a person needs to talk to someone straight away, the NHS has a mental health helpline page on its website which gives numbers of organisations covering virtually every mental health condition. This information is also listed at the back of this book under useful information.

In the first instance, when seeking help for a condition, a GP will make an assessment and offer advice and, if able to, treatment. They may also refer a person for help, for example psychological therapy or to a specialist mental health service within the NHS. The range of services may be provided by a GP or a larger local health centre, a specialist clinic dealing with mental health or a hospital. The treatment may be provided on a one to one basis, or, if appropriate in a group setting with others with similar conditions. Therapy can sometimes involve partners and families.

A person has a legal right to choose which service provider and clinical team they are referred to. Clinical Commissioning

Groups (CCG's) provide mental health services for their communities. A person has the right to choose any mental health service provider in England (if in England) as long as they provide a similar appropriate service to the one their local CCG provides. However, there are a number of situations where an individual does not have the legal right to choose, as follows:

o the service is not routinely provided by a local CCG – in this case, a person could ask their doctor to complete an individual funding request if they believe a particular treatment or service is the best treatment for them, given their individual clinical circumstances

o they need urgent or emergency treatment

o they already receive care and treatment for the condition they are being referred for

o the organisation or clinical team does not provide clinically appropriate care for their condition

o they are a prisoner, on temporary release from prison, or detained in other prescribed accommodation – such as a court, a secure children's home, a secure training centre, an immigration removal centre, or a young offender institution

o they are detained in a secure hospital setting

o they are a serving member of the armed forces

o they are detained under the Mental Health Act 1983.

The NHS Choices website www.nhs.uk provides a service where people can compare mental health service providers using the 'Services near you' tool. Once a person chooses a provider, they have the right to choose the team that will provide the appropriate service for them. This can be achieved through a GP, online (using a request letter from the GP) or by phoning the NHS e referral service on their helpline (see useful information). 75% of people referred to the Improved Access to Psychological Therapies (IAPT) programme will be treated within six weeks of referral, and 95% will be treated within 18 weeks of referral.

More than 50% of people experiencing a first episode of psychosis will be treated with a NICE-approved care package within two weeks of referral.

Child and adolescent mental health services (CAMHS)

CAMHS is a term for all services that work with children and young people who have difficulties with their emotional or behavioural wellbeing. Local areas have a number of different support services available. These might be from the statutory, voluntary or school-based sector, such as an NHS trust, local authority, school or charitable organisation.

Children and young people may need help with a wide range of issues at different points in their lives. Parents and carers may also need help and advice to deal with behavioural or other problems their child is experiencing.

Specialist CAMHS

Specialist CAMHS are NHS mental health services that focus on the needs of children and young people. They are multidisciplinary teams that often consist of:

- o psychiatrists
- o psychologists
- o social workers
- o nurses
- o support workers
- o occupational therapists
- o psychological therapists – this may include child psychotherapists, family psychotherapists, play therapists and creative art therapists
- o primary mental health link workers
- o specialist substance misuse workers

Getting help from specialist CAMHS

Getting help from a specialist CAMHS service is different depending on where a person lives. Waiting times can vary, too. Most CAHMS have their own website, which will have information about access, referrals and more, including phone numbers.

CAMHS information for parents and carers

If a parent is worried about a child or needs advice and support for coping with anything affecting a child's emotional or mental health, there are different ways to seek help.

NHS Choices offers information about services that provide mental health support for young people in addition, general advice and support can also be found online such as:

YoungMinds

YoungMinds offers free confidential online and telephone support to anyone worried about the emotional and mental wellbeing of a child or young person up to the age of 25. See back of the book for contact information.

MindEd

MindEd is an online e-portal offering free, simple advice to help adults identify, understand and support children and young people with mental health issues. Although it is aimed at professionals, parents and carers may also find the information helpful.

****

PART THREE

THE LAW AND MENTAL HEALTH

Chapter 6

The Mental Capacity Act 2005 (England and Wales) The Mental Capacity Acts Northern Ireland and Scotland.

The Mental Capacity Act 2005 (MCA) (England and Wales) is designed to protect and empower individuals who may lack the mental capacity to make their own decisions about their care and treatment. It is a law that applies to people of 16 and over. Conditions where people might lack mental capacity include: dementia; a severe learning disability; a brain injury; a mental health condition; a stroke or unconsciousness caused by an anaesthetic or sudden accident

Someone can lack capacity to make some decisions (for example, to decide on complex financial issues) but still have the capacity to make other less complex decisions

.

The Mental Capacity Act 2005 provides that:

o Everyone has the right to make his or her own decisions. Health and care professionals should always assume an individual has the capacity to make a decision themselves, unless it is proved otherwise through a capacity assessment. In addition, individuals must be given help to make a decision themselves.

o Where someone is judged not to have the capacity to make a specific decision (following a capacity assessment), that decision can be taken for them, but it must be in their best interests.

o Treatment and care provided to someone who lacks capacity should be the least restrictive of their basic rights and freedoms possible, while still providing the required treatment and care.

The MCA also allows people to express their preferences for care and treatment in case they lack capacity to make these decisions. It allows them to appoint a trusted person to make a decision on their behalf should they lack capacity in the future.

People should also be provided with an independent advocate who will support them to make decisions in certain situations, such as serious treatment or where the individual might have significant restrictions placed on their freedom and rights in their best interests.

How 'mental capacity' is determined

The MCA sets out a two-stage test of capacity.

1) Does the individual concerned have an impairment of, or a disturbance in the functioning of, their mind or brain, whether as a result of a condition, illness, or external factors such as alcohol or drug use?

2) Does the impairment or disturbance mean the individual is unable to make a specific decision when they need to? Individuals can lack capacity to make some decisions but have capacity to make others, so it is vital to consider whether the individual lacks capacity to make the specific decision.

Also, capacity can fluctuate with time – an individual may lack capacity at one point in time, but may be able to make the same decision at a later point in time. Where appropriate, individuals should be allowed the time to make a decision themselves. The MCA says a person is unable to make a decision if they cannot:

- understand the information relevant to the decision
- retain that information
- use or weigh up that information as part of the process of making the decision

If they aren't able to do any of the above three things or communicate their decision (by talking, using sign language, or through any other means), the MCA says they will be treated as unable to make the specific decision in question.

Mental capacity and supporting decision-making

Before deciding an individual lacks capacity to make a particular decision, appropriate steps must be taken to enable them to make the decision themselves.

Making best interests decisions for someone

If someone is found to lack the capacity to make a decision and such a decision needs to be made for them, the MCA states the decision must be made in their best interests.

Finding alternatives to making a decision on someone else's behalf

Before somebody makes a decision or acts on behalf of a person who lacks capacity to make a decision or to consent to an act, they must always question if they can do something else that would interfere less with the person's basic rights and freedoms. This is called finding the "least restrictive alternative". It includes considering whether there is a need to act or make a decision at all.

Where there is more than one option, it is important to explore ways that would be less restrictive or allow the most freedom for a person who lacks capacity. However, the final decision must always allow the original purpose of the decision or act to be achieved.

Any decision or action must still be in the best interests of the person who lacks capacity. So sometimes it may be necessary to choose an option that is not the least restrictive alternative if that option is in the person's best interests.

Deprivation of liberty

In certain cases, the restrictions placed upon an individual who lacks capacity to consent to the arrangements of their care may amount to "deprivation of liberty". This must be judged on a case-by-case basis. Where it appears a deprivation of liberty might occur, the provider of care (usually a hospital or a care home) has to apply to their local authority, who will then arrange an assessment of the individual's care and treatment to decide if the deprivation of liberty is in the best interests of the individual concerned. If it is, the local authority will grant a legal authorisation. If it is not, the care and treatment package must be changed – otherwise, an unlawful deprivation of liberty will occur. This system is known as the Deprivation of Liberty Safeguards.

Advance statements and decisions

An advance statement is a written statement that sets down a person's preferences, wishes, beliefs and values regarding their future care. It is not legally binding.

The aim is to provide a guide for anyone who might have to make decisions in someone's best interests if they have lost the capacity to make decisions or communicate their decision.

An advance statement can cover any aspect of a person's future health or social care.

Lasting Powers of Attorney (LPA)

A Person can grant a Lasting Power of Attorney (LPA) to another person (or people) to enable them to make decisions about health and welfare, or decisions about property and financial affairs. Separate legal documents are made for each of these decisions, appointing one or more attorneys for each.

An Enduring Power of Attorney (EPA) under the previous law was restricted to making decisions over just property and financial affairs. An EPA made before the Mental Capacity Act came into force on October 1 2007 remains valid.

Powers of attorney can be made at any time when the person making it has the mental capacity to do so, provided they are 18 or over. Both an EPA and LPA must be registered. An LPA can be registered at any time, but a personal welfare LPA will only be effective once the person has lost the capacity to make their own decisions.

The Court of Protection will be able to appoint deputies who can also take decisions on health and welfare, as well as in financial matters, if the person concerned lacks the capacity to make a decision. They will come into action when the court needs to delegate an ongoing series of decisions rather than one decision. If the person concerned already has an LPA appointed, they won't normally need a deputy as well.

The Office of the Public Guardian registers LPAs and EPAs and supervises court-appointed deputies. It provides evidence to the Court of Protection and information and guidance to the public. The Public Guardian works with a range of agencies, such as the financial sector, police and social services, to investigate concerns.

The Court of Protection (COP)

The COP make decisions on financial or welfare matters for people who can't make decisions at the time they need to be made (they 'lack mental capacity'). It is responsible for:

o deciding whether someone has the mental capacity to make a particular decision for themselves

o appointing deputies to make ongoing decisions for people who lack mental capacity

o giving people permission to make one-off decisions on behalf of someone else who lacks mental capacity o handling urgent or emergency applications where a decision must be made on behalf of someone else without delay

o making decisions about a lasting power of attorney or enduring power of attorney and considering any objections to their registration

o considering applications to make statutory wills or gifts

o making decisions about when someone can be deprived of their liberty under the Mental Capacity Act

Professionals' duties under the Mental Capacity Act

The Mental Capacity Act applies to all professions – doctors, nurses, social workers, occupational therapists, health care assistants, and support staff. These staff and their employers have a duty to ensure they are trained in its implementation.

All staff working in the NHS and in social care are expected to have an understanding of the act as it relates to their own responsibilities. Most trusts and local authorities will have a Mental Capacity Act lead who provides specialist advice on the implementation.

Mental Capacity Scotland-Adults with Incapacity (Scotland) Act 2000

The Act covers the system for safeguarding the welfare, and managing the finances and property, of adults (aged 16 or over)

who lack the capacity to take some or all decisions for themselves because of mental disorder or inability to communicate by any means. It allows other people to make decisions on behalf of these adults, subject to safeguards.

Main principles

All decisions made on behalf of an adult with impaired capacity must:

- Benefit the adult
- take account of the adult's past and present wishes
- restrict the adult's freedom as little as possible while still achieving the desired benefit
- encourage the adult to use existing skills or develop new skills
- take account of the views of others with an interest in the adult's welfare.

Under the Act a number of different agencies are involved in supervising those who take decisions on behalf of the adult.

- the Public Guardian has a supervisory role and keeps registers of attorneys, people who can access an adult's funds, guardians and intervention orders
- local authorities look after the welfare of adults who lack capacity

o the Mental Welfare Commission protects the interests of adults who lack capacity as a result of mental disorder

Under the Act, the main ways that other people can make decisions for an adult with impaired capacity are:

Power of Attorney

Individuals can arrange for their welfare to be safeguarded and their affairs to be properly managed in future, should their capacity deteriorate. They can do this by giving another person (who could be a relative, carer, professional person or trusted friend) power of attorney to look after some or all of their property and financial affairs and/or to make specified decisions about their personal welfare, including medical treatment.

Access to the adult's funds

Individuals (normally relatives or carers) can apply to the Public Guardian to gain access to the funds of an adult incapable of managing those funds. This applies to funds held in, for example, a bank or building society account in the sole name of the adult.

The Act also includes provisions to allow access to a joint account to continue where one account holder has become incapable of managing the funds.

Funds of residents in care establishments

Authorised care establishments can manage a limited amount of the funds and property of residents who are unable to do this themselves.

Medical treatment and research

The Act allows treatment to be given to safeguard or promote the physical or mental health of an adult who is unable to consent. Special provisions apply where others such as attorneys have been appointed under the Act with powers relating to medical treatment. Where there is disagreement a second medical opinion can be sought. Cases can also be referred to the Court of Session in certain circumstances. The Act also permits research involving an adult incapable of giving consent but only under strict guidelines.

Intervention and guardianship orders

Individuals can apply to their local Sheriff Court for:

- an intervention order where a one-off decision or short-term help is required (for example selling property or signing a document)
- a guardianship order, which may be more appropriate where the continuous management of affairs or the safeguarding of welfare is required.

Local authorities or any person claiming an interest in the adult's affairs may make applications for intervention and guardianship orders.

The Mental Capacity Act (Northern Ireland) 2016

This Act came in to force in March 2016. The Act contains High Court powers to make decisions for vulnerable individuals. It provides for the Police Service of Northern Ireland to remove a vulnerable person to a place of safety so that appropriate medical attention can be provided, and it facilitates the transfer to hospital of individuals who are subject to criminal proceedings or those who are detained in the criminal justice system.

"These powers respect a person's right to make decisions about whether they wish to receive healthcare treatment, whilst ensuring that the criminal justice system continues to have robust mechanisms for safeguarding public protection."

The Act is principles-based. The principles are set out at the start and underpin the entire legislation: First Principle: capacity. A person is not to be treated as lacking capacity unless it is established that the person lacks capacity in relation to a matter. The person is not to be treated as unable to make a decision for himself or herself about the matter unless all practicable help and support to enable the person to make a decision about the matter have been given without success.

The person is not to be treated as unable to make a decision for himself or herself about the matter merely because the person makes an unwise decision. Second Principle: best interests. The act must be done, or the decision must be made, in the person's best interests. The person making the determination must have special regard to the person's past and present wishes and feelings, the beliefs and values that would be likely to influence their decision if they had capacity and any other factors that thy would be likely to consider if able to do so.

****

Chapter 7

The Respective Mental Health Acts -England and Wales, Scotland and Northern Ireland

---

England and Wales

The 1983 Mental Health Act, (MHA) as amended by the 2007 MHA, is the law in England and Wales that allows people with a mental disorder to be admitted to hospital and detained and treated without their consent. This is for both their own safety and the safety of other people.

The Human Rights Act 1998. This important piece of legislation underpins the safeguards and rights of all individuals, including those with a mental disorder. All public authorities, including mental health professionals and others tasked to carry out functions under the Mental Health Act are required under domestic law to:

- o Interpret the Act as far as is possible to do so, in a way that is compatible with the European Convention of Human Rights (ECHR).

o Ensure that practice is guided by and compatible with the Human Rights Act 1998.

o Take account of relevant domestic and European case law in relation to these matters in their practice.

The individual rights and freedoms enshrined in the European Convention of Human Rights are now part of domestic law and enforceable in courts throughout the UK .

The Mental Health Act 1983 (as amended) is divided into sections, hence the term 'sectioning'. People are admitted and treated under different sections, depending on the circumstances. Section 2 is used to admit someone for assessment. Two doctors must agree that someone should be detained in hospital for treatment and one of them must be a section 12 approved doctor. An Approved Mental Health professional or someone's nearest relative can then apply to hospital managers for an individual to be admitted under Section 2. People admitted under Section 2 can be kept in hospital for 28 days. Section 2 cannot be renewed. If health professionals want to detain people longer they have to do so under Section 3.

Section 3 covers treatment and allows people to be admitted for treatment for up to six months. Again, 2 doctors have to agree someone to be detained for treatment, one of whom must be a Section 12 approved doctor. An AMHP or nearest relative can then apply to hospital managers for an individual to be admitted under Section 3.

A nearest relative must be consulted by an AMHP before a patient is admitted under Section 3 unless impracticable to do so or create an unreasonable delay. If the nearest relative objects then the admittance cannot go ahead unless a court order is obtained. A patients responsible clinician can renew Section 3 to keep them in hospital for longer than six months. They can also take the decision to discharge them under a Community Treatment Order (see below)

Section 4 deals with emergency and applies where there is a crisis and someone needs urgent help but there isn't enough time to arrange for an admission under Section 2 or 3. Section 4 allows for someone to be admitted and detained for up to 72 hours after one doctor has said that urgent admission is needed. An AMHP will usually make the application for a Section 4 admission.

If a person is admitted to hospital compulsorily they are known as 'formal' or 'involuntary patients.

The Mental Health Act also allows people to be put on what are known as Community Treatment Orders (CTO's) following a period of compulsory treatment in hospital.

Community Treatment Orders

People can be discharged from hospital under a Community Treatment Order (CTO) after being on a Section 3 or Section 37. The responsible clinician (see below) will take this decision with a supporting recommendation from an Approved Mental Health Professional. CTO's have conditions attached, which might include staying at a specific address, attending for treatment at specified times or taking medication as prescribed. If the person does not comply they may be recalled to hospital for up to 72 hours and an assessment will be made after the assessment then person may be allowed to go back to the community or readmitted with the original section coming back into force.

The decision to detain someone under S2 of the MHA 1983 or put someone on a CTO is taken by doctors and also other mental health professionals who are approved to carry out certain duties under the Act and they are subject to specific procedures. In addition to doctors and mental health professionals the Crown Court can issue an order for compulsory admittance to hospital. Magistrates can also issue an order for an assessment only.

Detention of voluntary patients

If a person is admitted to hospital on a voluntary basis, then they are known as Informal or Voluntary patients. They are not detained as they admitted themselves voluntarily. However, under Section 5 (2) a doctor can stop them leaving hospital. This is done only if the doctor thinks that they pose a risk to their own and other health and safety. the section 5(2) lasts for up to 72 hours, giving time to consider other options.

In certain cases, if a doctor is not available then a registered nurse can use Section 5(4) to prevent someone leaving hospital. This power lasts for up to six hours and ends when a doctor arrives on the ward.

Leave of absence when detained in hospital

Section 117 of the Mental Health Act covers leave of absence for those detained in hospital. It is against the law for someone to leave hospital without the permission of the responsible clinician. When people are detained in hospital under Sections 2,3 and 37 they may be given a time limited leave of absence to visit family (for example) or for a visit home prior to discharge.

Section 12 approved doctors and approved mental health professionals

An approved mental health professional (AMHP is a social worker, mental health nurse, occupational therapist or a social worker who has been specifically trained to carry out certain duties under the Mental Health Act by an organisation acting on behalf of the Secretary of State in England or Welsh Ministers in Wales). These professionals receive approval for five years at a time. However, only an approved clinician can take overall responsibility for the case of someone who has been detained in hospital or on a CTO and act as their 'responsible clinician'. Almost all responsible clinicians are, currently, doctors.

A doctor who is 'approved' under Section 12 of the Act is approved on behalf of the Secretary of State (or the Welsh Ministers) as being expert in the diagnosis and treatment of mental disorders. Doctors who are approved clinicians are automatically approved under Section 12. Doctors approved under Section 12 have a key role in the decisions as to whether someone should be detained under section 2 and Section 3 of the MHA.

The Mental Health Act Code of Practice

As might be expected, there is a clear code of practice with the 1983 Mental Health Act (as amended). This Code of Practice contains guidelines that health professionals should follow when detaining and treating people under the Mental Health Act. In 2015, a revised and updated Code of Practice came into effect, which reflected changes in professional practice since the last update in 2008. The Code of Practice contains guiding principles that mental health professionals should consider when taking decisions to detain and treat people under the Mental Health Act.

One of the main guiding principles is that a person who is being detained and treated against their will should be as fully involved as it is possible to be in their treatment plan and their wishes taken into account and respected by mental health professionals. Family members and other people such as carers will also be involved unless the person who is being treated does not want them to be.

Another key guiding principle is that care and treatment of the person being detained should be provided in the least restrictive way possible.

The role of hospital managers

The Mental Health Act describes as 'Hospital Managers' the organisation that is in charge of the hospital, for example the NHS Trust. Hospital managers are responsible, ultimately, for what happens to people who are detained and treated under the MHA in a particular hospital. They are responsible for making sure that the law is adhered to and also that patients are informed of their rights.

Patients appeals are heard by hospital managers, for example those patients who disagree with a decision to detain them. They can discharge patients who have been detained (although not patients who have been detained by the courts or who are on a Community Treatment Order.

Identifying the nearest relative

When someone is detained under the Mental Health Act, the Approved Mental Health Professional has a responsibility to identify the persons nearest relative. The law states that the nearest relative is someone's husband, wife, civil partner or unmarried partner if they have been living together for more than six months. there will always be circumstances where someone does not have any of the above. the next nearest relative will be a child, if they are over 18 years of age. If there is no child then one of the parents is next in line. If both parents are dead then there is a further 'pecking order' of those over 18: brothers and sisters, grandparents, grandchild, uncle or aunt, nephew or niece or somebody who is not related but with whom the person has lived for more than five years. The Mental Health Act confers powers on the chosen nearest relative.

The nearest relative must be informed, for S2, or consulted (S3) if mental health professionals are proposing to detain someone for treatment under the Act. This is only the case if it is practicable to do so or unless consultation would cause unreasonable delays A patient cannot be admitted under Section 3 if the nearest relative disagrees with the decision although they can be over ridden if the professional decides to get a court order.

In addition, the nearest relative can apply to the hospital managers to admit someone to hospital compulsorily for assessment (Section 2) or Treatment (Section 3), or in an emergency (Section 4). The nearest relative can also ask the hospital managers to discharge the person who has been detained (unless it is through a court order). However, this can be blocked if it is thought that the person poses a risk.

Powers of the courts to intervene

The Crown Court and the Magistrates Court can use the Mental Health Act to either send someone to treatment or commission a report into their mental health. Section 35 of the MHA is used to send an accused on remand to hospital for a report and Section 36 used to send a person for treatment.

Under Section 37, a court can rule that someone convicted of an offence be sent to hospital for treatment rather than prison. If the courts are concerned that the person poses a risk to others then Section 41 allows for a restriction order to be added. Section 38 allows for someone convicted of an offence to be sent to hospital for an assessment before sentencing.

The Mental Health Act allows for both convicted prisoners and those on remand to be transferred to a hospital for treatment. Section 47 is used to transfer a sentenced prisoner to hospital and section 48 for a prisoner on remand. A restriction order under Section 49 is usually attached.

Police powers

Police powers in relation to mental health are defined by Section 136 of the Mental Health Act 1983, as amended. Section 136 allows the police to remove someone from a public place to a place of safety. This can happen if the police think that the person needs immediate care. A place of safety would be a mental hospital, accident and emergency department or a police cell. A person can be held for up to 72 hours during which time they should be seen by a doctor and an Approved Mental Health Professional. Following on from this they can then be placed on a Section 2 or 3 of the Mental Health Act, admitted to hospital as an informal or formal patient or discharged.

Section 135 of the MHA allows the police to gain entry into someone's premises to allow a mental health assessment to be made or to return someone to hospital who has not returned. A warrant from a magistrates court is needed before the powers under section 135 can be used. For patients who are to be assessed for detention an Approved Mental Health Professional must be in attendance. The Mental Health Code of Practice contains guidance for the use of police powers.

Guardianship

Section 7 of the Mental Health Act allows for people who have a mental illness to be given a guardian who will act in the interests of the person affected and also other people. The fundamental role of a guardian is to help a person to live in the community as independently as possible. If a person is detained in hospital under the MHA they may be discharged to receive care and treatment under guardianship.

The guardian is typically the local authority but can be an individual who is approved by the local authority (termed a 'private guardian') Medical recommendations from two doctors are needed and then the approved mental health worker, or a nearest relative, can apply to the Local authority for a guardianship order to be made. However, if there is an objection from a nearest relative to the making of a guardianship order then it cannot be made. Courts can also make guardianship orders under Section 37 of the MHA.

The Mental Health Act Section 8 confers powers on the guardian to require a person to live in a certain place, to require a person to attend appointments for treatment, occupation or training and to require a doctor or approved mental health professional to visit. However, guardianship does not allow treatment to be given without a persons consent.

A guardianship order lasts for up to six months in the first instance but can be renewed for a year at a time. The local authority will consult a doctor before renewing.

A person can ask to stop having a guardian by writing to the local authority or the First Tier Tribunal (Mental Health) see below.

Right to appeal against decisions made under the Mental Health Act

When a person is compulsorily admitted for treatment the hospital managers have a duty to inform them of their rights to appeal against detention. There are no rights to appeal against short term detentions (very short term) but for longer term detentions a person can appeal to hospital managers and also to the First Tier Tribunals (Mental Health)or Mental Health Tribunal for Wales. People on a Community Treatment Order also have the same right of appeal. Ward staff must inform patients of their rights in this respect and how to contact the various parties. Independent health advocates can also help patients understand their rights. Local authorities will organise Independent Advocates.

After leaving hospital

Section 117 of the Mental Health Act provides for free aftercare for people who have been detained and given treatment under Sections 3, 37, 47 or 48. This includes those people who have been discharged onto supervised community treatment. NHS clinical commissioning groups and local social services are responsible for providing and paying for aftercare, The Mental Health Code of Practice gives examples of aftercare which can include assistance with employment and accommodation. The patient should be involved in aftercare along with a relative unless the patient does not want the involvement of a relative. Aftercare services under Section 117 will continue until the section is formally discharged.

The role of the Care Quality Commission.

The Care Quality Commission (CQC) is the independent regulator for health and social care in England. It makes sure services such as hospitals, care homes, dentists and GP surgeries provide people with safe, effective, compassionate and high-quality care, and encourages these services to improve. The CQC monitors and inspects these services, and then publishes its findings and ratings to help people make choices about their care. The CQC carries out its role in the following ways:

- o Making sure services meet fundamental standards of quality and safety that people have a right to expect whenever they receive care.
- o Registering care service providers that are able to show they will meet these standards.
- o Monitoring, inspecting and regulating care services to make sure they continue to meet the standards.
- o Protecting the rights of vulnerable people, including those whose rights are restricted under the Mental Health Act.
- o Listening to and acting on your experiences.

- o Involving people who use services.

- o Working in partnership with other organisations and local groups.

- o Challenging all providers, with the worst performers getting the most attention.

- o Making fair and authoritative judgements supported by the best information and evidence.

- o Taking appropriate action if care services are failing to meet the fundamental standards.

- o Carrying out in-depth reviews to look at care across the system.

- o Reporting on the quality of care, including ratings to help people choose services.

CQC inspections and ratings

CQC inspection teams are made up of clinical and other experts, as well as people with direct experience of the relevant type of care. The teams visit services, speak to staff and patients, and observe the care provided. Each service is assessed against five key questions:

- o Is it safe?
- o Is it effective?
- o Is it caring?
- o Is it responsive to people's needs?
- o Is it well led?

Based on the outcome of the inspection, CQC gives an overall rating as well as one for each of the key questions. Further ratings for core services (such as surgery or maternity in hospitals) or population groups (such as people with long-term conditions in GP services) can also be awarded.

There are four levels of rating:

- **outstanding** – the service is performing exceptionally well
- **good** – the service is performing well and meets CQC's expectations
- **requires improvement** – the service isn't performing as well as it should and CQC has told the service how it should improve
- **inadequate** – the service is performing badly and CQC has taken action against the person or organisation that runs it

The Care Quality Commission is responsible for protecting the interests of people detained and treated under the Mental Health Act in England, for making sure they are cared for properly, and for ensuring the Mental Health Act is used correctly. It does this by monitoring the use of the Mental Health Act, and by visiting hospitals and speaking to patients. The Care Quality Commission appoints 'Mental Health Act commissioners' who visit every psychiatric ward in England where patients are detained on a regular basis. They also seek to meet patients placed on supervised community treatment. In Wales, The Healtcare Review inspectorate is responsible for monitoring the Mental Health Act. Their 'Mental Health Act reviewers' visit psychiatric wards and meet patients placed on supervised community treatment.

Scotland -Mental Health Law in Scotland

The law relating to Mental Health in Scotland is the Mental Health (Care and Treatment) (Scotland) Act 2003. This Act enables medical professionals to detain and treat people against their will on grounds of mental disorder. The Mental Health Tribunal for Scotland and the Mental Welfare Commission for Scotland provide safeguards against mistreatment. The Act is designed to ensure that free and informed consent forms the basis of treatment for people experiencing mental health problems. It creates provisions for people to participate in decisions relating to their care wherever possible.

Advocacy

The Act gives every person with a mental health problem a right of access to independent advocacy. It puts duties on Health Boards and Local Authorities to ensure that independent advocacy services are available. This right to access advocacy applies to *everyone* with a mental health problem, not just to people who are subject to powers under the Act.

Advance statements

People have a right to make advance statements, setting out how they would wish to be treated if they become unwell and unable to express their views clearly. The Mental Health Tribunal and any person responsible for giving treatment under the Act must take an advance statement into account.

Named persons

Service users aged 16 or over, can choose someone, referred to as a 'named person', to support them and to protect their interests in any proceedings under the Act. The named person has the same rights as the service user to be notified of, attend and be represented at Mental Health Tribunal hearings.

The Mental Health Tribunal

The Act established the Mental Health Tribunal to be involved in consideration of care plans, decisions on compulsory treatment orders and to carry out reviews. Service users and carers have a right to challenge compulsory treatment orders if they want to, and the Tribunal must listen to their views and make any decisions fairly and impartially.

Compulsory Treatment Orders

These have to be approved by a Tribunal. The patient, the patient's named person and the patient's primary carer are entitled to have any objections that they have heard by the

Tribunal. The patient and the named person are also entitled to free legal representation for the Tribunal hearing.

Other safeguards

There are other safeguards in the Act. Some of these will benefit all mental health service users, not just people who are treated under the Act. These include:

o A right for service users and carers to request an assessment of the service user's needs. Both Health Boards and Local Authorities will have a duty to respond to a request for assessment within 14 days. If they refuse a request for assessment, they will have to give reasons for their decision.

o Duties on local authorities to provide 'care and support services' and 'services designed to promote well-being and social development' for people who have, or have had, a mental disorder. Some examples of these include residential accommodation, home support, training and assistance in obtaining employment and social activities.

The Mental Health (Care and Treatment) Scotland Act 2003 sets out when can a person be taken into hospital and given treatment against their will. It also describes what their rights are and puts in place safeguards to make sure rights are protected. Any mental health service user can use the Act to ensure that they are receiving care and support which is appropriate to their needs.

The Mental Welfare Commission has a vital role in protecting the rights of service users and promoting the effective operation of the new Act. This includes: monitoring how the Act is working; encouraging best practice; publishing information and guidance; carrying out visits to patients and conducting investigations.

Northern Ireland

In Northern Ireland, mental health issues are covered by the Mental Health (Northern Ireland) Order 1986. This Order covers the assessment, treatment and rights of people with a mental health condition.

The Mental Health (Northern Ireland) Order 1986

In most situations people will choose whether or not to seek help for their mental disorder and will do so voluntarily. They will have the right to accept or decline care and treatments, to choose to be treated in hospital or in the community, to leave hospital at any time and to live independently and without interference in the community.

The Order provides a framework for the care, treatment and protection of all persons with a mental disorder and establishes systems through which the statutory rights of individuals and their relatives are protected and the duties, responsibilities and powers of professionals regulated. The powers and protections set out in the legislation apply to all persons with a mental disorder in Northern Ireland, adults and children, regardless of whether they are a resident in the jurisdiction or not.

The Order also contains provisions in relation to some individuals who may, because of the nature and degree of their mental disorder, place themselves and or/others at risk. When this occurs, and when the individual is deemed to be unable or unwilling to accept care and treatment, the law places a responsibility on certain health and social care professionals and others to intervene.

Provisions contained within the Order

The first part of the Order (Part 1) is concerned with definitions

- o **Part II** of the Order is specifically concerned with providing a legal framework for the compulsory admission for assessment and detention in hospital for treatment of mental disorder and with Reception into Guardianship.
- o **Part III** contains separate provisions for those persons with a mental disorder concerned in criminal proceedings or under sentence by a court.
- o **Part IV** sets out the law on consent to treatment for mental disorder.

o **Parts V and Part VI** of the Order are primarily concerned with protections for persons with a mental disorder. **Part V** sets out the role of the Mental Health Review Tribunal in protecting against unjustified detention or Guardianship. **Part VI** established the Mental Health Commission with a broad remit to oversee the care, treatment and protection of all individuals with a mental disorder. This function has since been transferred to the Regulation and Quality Improvement Authority (RQIA).

o **Part VII** is concerned with the Registration of Private Hospitals.

o **Part VIII** is concerned with the Management of Property and Affairs of Patients.

o **Part IX** Sets out the Miscellaneous Functions of the Department and Boards/ Trusts, including the statutory duty on Trusts to appoint a sufficient number of approved Social Workers for the purposes of discharging the functions conferred on them in the Order.

o **Part X** is concerned with Offences.

o **Part XI** addresses Miscellaneous and Supplementary matters.

Two guidance documents were produced in 1986 and 1992:

- **A Guide** (published 1986) Department of Health and Social Services (NI)
- **Code of Practice** (published (1992) - Department of Health and Social Services

While the Mental Health (Northern Ireland) Order 1986 sets out statutory rights, powers and responsibilities, the Guide and the Code of Practice to the Mental Health (Northern Ireland) Order 1986 contain guidance for medical practitioners, Health and Social Care Trusts, hospital staff, approved social workers and others in relation to the admission of patients to hospitals and treatment of persons with a mental disorder and the reception of individuals into Guardianship.

The Code of practice contains a list of specific principles in relation to treatment. **5.3** of the Code of Practice states that all treatment should:

- **Be primarily for the benefit of the patient.** Where possible the patient's willing participation should be obtained. The main aims should be, so far as possible, to improve health and reduce handicap including social handicap;
- **Protect the safety of the patient and other people**. In the course of treatment or in the interests of safety, restriction of liberty may be necessary but should never be

used as a punishment and should only be used as a last resort to the minimum extent necessary;

o **Respect the patient's dignity and rights.** No treatment should deprive a patient of food, shelter, water, warmth, a comfortable environment or confidentiality;

o **Respect the patient's rights to privacy and freedom of choice.** Forms of treatment, such as psychological treatment techniques, group therapy and behaviour modification programmes, which may intrude on the patient's normal right to privacy and freedom of action, should be carefully planned and conducted by experienced and appropriately trained staff and should be kept under review;

o **Respect the patient's rights to information.** Patients are entitled to information and explanation about their condition, and treatment which is proposed, and their rights. This information should be conveyed at a suitable time and in a form which takes account of the patient's capacity to understand. These principles apply to the treatment of all mentally disordered patients whether or not they are in hospital. In hospital practice they apply to both voluntary and detained patients including those admitted under Part III of the Order.

This means, in particular, that all individuals should be as fully involved as practicable, consistent with their needs and wishes, in the formulation and delivery of their care and treatment. They should be informed about the nature, purpose and likely outcome of any proposed treatment. This applies equally to young patients and to patients who are receiving care or treatment on a compulsory basis.

Where physical difficulties such as hearing impairment impede such involvement, reasonable steps should be taken to attempt to overcome them. It means that patients should have their legal rights drawn to their attention, consistent with their capacity to understand them. Where they cannot understand, their rights should be explained to their carers, relatives or friends as appropriate.

A number of pieces of legislation and policy documents should also be considered when carrying out duties and responsibilities under the Order. These include:

The Human Rights Act 1998.

This important piece of legislation underpins the safeguards and rights of all individuals, including those with a mental disorder. All public authorities, including mental health professionals and others tasked to carry out functions under the Mental Health (Northern Ireland) Order 1986 are now required under domestic law to:

o Interpret the Order, as far as is possible to do so, in a way that is compatible with the European Convention of Human Rights (ECHR).

o Ensure that practice is guided by and compatible with the Human Rights Act 1998.

o Take account of relevant domestic and European case law in relation to these matters in their practice.

As stated at the beginning of this chapter, the individual rights and freedoms enshrined in the European Convention of Human Rights are now part of domestic law and enforceable in courts throughout the UK including NI courts.

****

Resource Section-Useful Information

General

Mental Health Foundation

Provides information and support for anyone with mental health problems or learning disabilities.

Website: www.mentalhealth.org.uk

NHS. UK

This is the website of the National Health Service and is the starting point for information about all aspects of health including mental health and the services offered.

Rethink.org.uk

This is the website of rethink mental illness and is extremely comprehensive. It covers everything to do with all aspects of mental illness, including the law, different conditions and benefits advice plus wills and trusts, advice for carers and friends and financial matters generally.

Samaritans

www.samaritans.org.uk

Phone 116 123 (free 24 hour helpline)

Confidential support for people experiencing feelings of despair.

SANE

Charity offering support and carrying out research into mental illness.

Phone: 0300 304 7000 (daily, 4.30-10.30 pm)

SANEmail email: sanemail@org.uk

Website: www.sane.org.uk

YoungMinds

Information on child and adolescent mental health. Services for parents and professionals. Phone: Parents' helpline 0808 802 5544 (Mon-Fri, 9.30am-4pm)

Website: www.youngminds.org.uk

Anxiety

Anxiety UK

A user led organisation that supports anyone with anxiety, phobias, panic attacks or other anxiety related disorders. They can be contacted at:

Telephone: 08444 775 774 or 0161 227 9898

Email: info@anxietyuk.org.uk

Website: www.anxietyuk.org.uk

Anxiety Alliance

A charity dedicated to helping those suffering from anxiety.

Telephone: 0345 2967877

Email: harris835@btinternet.com

Website: www.anxietyalliance.org.uk

SASH (London Social Anxiety Self-Help Groups)

Run groups across the London area.

Email: info@sashgroup.org

Website: www.sashgroup.org

Social Anxiety UK

Offers support with social anxiety disorder. They are a web-based organisation and offer forums, a chatroom and information on the condition.

Email: contact@social-anxiety.org.uk

Website: www.social-anxiety.org.uk

OCD-UK

Gives information, advice and support on obsessive compulsive disorder (OCD) and related disorders .

Telephone: 03332 127890

Email: support@ocduk.org

Website: www.ocduk.org

Combat Stress

Offers support for veterans who have been involved in military combat and have symptoms of PTSD.

Telephone: 0800 138 1619

Email: contactus@combatstress.org.uk

Website: www.combatstress.org.uk

No Panic

Offers emotional support and information on anxiety disorders and medication including tranquilizers.

Telephone: 0844 967 4848

Youth Helpline: 01753 840393 (For 13 to 20 year olds)

Email: admin@nopanic.org.uk

Website: www.nopanic.org.uk

Bi-Polar

Bipolar UK

This is a user led charity working to enable people affected by bipolar disorder to take control of their lives

Telephone: 0333 323 3880

Email: info@bipolaruk.org.uk

Website: www.bipolaruk.org.uk/

Depression

Depression Alliance

This service runs self help groups across the country.

Email: information@depressionalliance.org

Website: www.depressionalliance.org

Friend in Need

Friends in Need is a way for people affected by depression to meet online and in their local area. It's free to join.

Website: https://friendsinneed.co.uk/

Mood Swings Network

This service provides a range of services for people affected by mood disorders such as depression and includes family and friends.

Telephone: 0161 832 37 36

Email: info@moodswings.org.uk Website: www.moodswings.org.uk

The Conservation Volunteers

This organisation helps people to get involved in local conservation projects.

Website: www.tcv.org.uk/

Do-it

This is an organisation that supports people to get into volunteering across the country.

Website: https://do-it.org/

Eating disorders

Anorexia and Bulimia Care

An organisation that provides on-going care, emotional support and practical guidance for anyone affected by eating disorders.

Helpline: 03000 11 12 13

Email: support@anorexiabulimiacare.org.uk

Website: www.anorexiabulimiacare.org.uk

Beat (formerly the Eating Disorders Association UK)

A national charity based in the UK providing information, help and support for people affected by eating disorders.

tel: 0808 801 0677

Website: www.b-eat.co.uk

Youthline

For anyone under 25. Open 2-4pm Monday to Friday.

Telephone: 01344 311200

Text service: 07786201820

Email: fyp@b-eat.co.uk

Eating Disorders and Carers

Runs the London Carers' Group, a self help group run by and for carers of those with an eating disorder. 07733 260 475

Website: www.eatingdisordersandcarers.co.uk

Eating Disorders Support

An organisation that provides help and support to anyone affected by an eating problem.

Helpline: 01494 793223

Email: support@eatingdisorderssupport.co.uk

Website: www.eatingdisorderssupport.co.uk

National Centre for Eating Disorders

An independent organisation set up to provide solutions for all eating problems, compulsive or "binge" eating, failed or "yo-yo" dieting, bulimia and anorexia. They provide information and counselling.

Telephone: 0845 838 2040

Address: National Centre for Eating Disorders, 54 New Road, Esher, Surrey KT10 9NU

Website: www.eating-disorders.org.uk

The Recover Clinic

Provides care and advice for those suffering with eating disorders including Anorexia, Bulimia and Compulsive Overeating, Orthorexia, and Body Dysmorphic Disorder.

Telephone: 0845 603 6530

Email: help@therecoverclinic.co.uk

Website: www.therecoverclinic.co.uk

SEED (Support and Empathy for people with Eating Disorders)

Charity offering advice, support and services to people in Hull East Riding and out of area.

Helpline: 01482 718130

Email: hello@seedeatingdisorders.org.uk

Website: http://www.seedeatingdisorders

Psychosis

The Royal College of Psychiatrists

This is an organization with a website that has information about a variety of mental illnesses that are associated with psychotic symptoms.

Telephone: 020 7235 2351

Email: reception@rcpsych.ac.uk

Website: http://www.rcpsych.ac.uk/

Voice Collective

This is an organization with a website that has information about voices, visions, coping, recovery, getting help in a crisis and peer support groups for young people aged 12 to 18. It also contains useful information for carers.

Telephone: 020 7911 0822

Email: info@voicecollective.co.uk

Website: www.voicecollective.co.uk

Post Traumatic Stress Disorder

Anxiety UK

User-led organisation which supports people with anxiety disorders, including PTSD.

Telephone: 03444 775 774 (Mon-Fri 9:30-17:30)

Website: www.anxietyuk.org.uk

ASSIST (Assistance Support and Self Help in Surviving Trauma)

Not-for-profit organisation offering therapists trained in trauma-focused CBT, EMDR and treating complex PTSD.

Telephone: 01788 560 800

Website: www.assisttraumacare.org.uk

Combat Stress

Charity offering support to ex-Service men and women of all ages with mental ill-health. Telephone: 0800 138 1619 (24 hours)

Email: contactus@combatstress.org.uk

Website: www.combatstress.org.uk

Freedom from Torture

Support, practical advice and treatment for survivors of torture. Has access to language interpreters.

Telephone: 020 7697 7777

Email: via website

Website: www.freedomfromtorture.org/

Rape Crisis

Support for survivors of rape and sexual assault.

Telephone: 0808 802 9999 (Helpline open 12:00-14:30 and 19:00-21:30 daily)

Email: rcewinfo@rapecrisis.org.uk (general enquiries)

Website: www.rapecrisis.org.uk

UK Psychological Trauma Society

Online list of UK trauma services.

Website: www.ukpts.co.uk/trauma.html

Veterans UK

Government body offering support for veterans.

Telephone: 0808 1914 218

Email: veterans-uk@mod.uk

Website: www.veterans-uk.info

****

Index

Advocacy, 128
Aggressive behaviour, 34
Agoraphobia, 6, 75
Alcohol, 14, 85
Amitriptyline, 44
Anticonvulsant drugs, 42
Anti-depressants, 43
Anti-parkinsonian drugs, 46
Antipsychotic drugs, 45
Antipsychotic Medications, 30
Antisocial personality disorder (ASPD), 80
Anxiety disorder, 5, 65
Appetit, 35
Approved Mental Health Professional, 116, 120, 122
Avoidant personality disorder, 82

Bipolar 1 disorder, 36
Bipolar 2 disorder, 36
Bi-Polar disorder, 17
Brain chemistry, 15
Brain damage, 5, 16, 63

Carbamazepine, 42, 43
Care co-ordinators, 49
Care Programme Approach (CPA), 47
Care Quality Commission (CQC, 125
Child and adolescent mental health services (CAMHS), 6, 94
Childhood bipolar disorder, 38, 40
Childhood bi-polar disorder, 38
Childhood distress, 38
Cognitive behavioral therapy, 48

Community mental health teams, 47
Community psychiatric nurse, 47
Community Treatment Orders, 7, 116
Concentration, 4, 35, 51, 52
Constipation, 51
Cortisol, 57
Counselling, 5, 48, 70
Crown Court, 116, 121
Cyclothymia, 36

Delusions, 4, 19, 25, 51, 52
Dementia, 84
Dependent personality disorder, 81
Depression, 4, 17, 33, 34, 37, 50, 55, 60, 83, 141
Depressive personality, 5, 64
Deprivation of liberty, 7, 103
Detention, 7, 116
Drugs, 42, 56, 78

Enduring Power of Attorney (EPA, 104

Family conflicts, 16
Family therapy, 48
Fatigue, 35

Generalized Anxiety Disorder, 73
Genetics, 78
Grief, 38
Group therapy, 48
Guardianship, 8, 122, 132, 133, 134

Hallucinations, 19, 24, 51, 52
Heart disease, 17

Histrionic personality disorder, 81
Hormones, 57
'Hospital Managers, 119
Hospitalization, 50
Human Rights Act 1998, 7, 113, 114, 136, 137
Hypomania, 4, 33, 34

Informal, 116
Irritability, 35

Juvenile depression, 5, 58

Lamotrigine, 42, 43
Largacti, 46
Lasting Powers of Attorney (LPA), 104
Leave of absence, 7, 117
Lithium, 42
Lithium carbonate, 42
Lithium Citrate, 42
Loss of appetite, 5, 54

Magistrates Court, 121
Manic episodes, 4, 33
Medication, 41, 42
Mental Capacity Act 2005 (MCA) (England and Wales, 99
Mental Capacity Scotland-Adults with Incapacity (Scotland) Act
    2000, 106
Mental Health (Care and Treatment) (Scotland) Act 2003, 128
Mental Health Act 1983, 93, 114, 122
Mental Health Act Code of Practice, 8, 118
Mental health care pathways, 6, 91
Mental health services, 6, 89, 90
Minor tranquillisers, 46

Mixed episode, 36
Mixed episodes, 33
Mood stabilisers, 70
Movement disorders, 26

Narcissistic personality disorder, 81
National Institute for Health and Care Excellence (NICE, 41
Nearest relative, 8, 120
Nerve cell releases, 5, 56
Neuroleptics, 45

Obsessive–compulsive disorder, 77
Older adults, 83
Osteoarthritis., 83

Paranoid personality disorder, 79
Parkinson's, 37
Phobias, 5, 74
Police powers, 8, 122
Post-traumatic stress disorder (PTSD), 62, 77
Poverty, 17
Prozac, 44
Psychodynamic therapists, 49
Psychoeducation, 48
Psychosis, 3, 17, 19, 20, 145
Psychosocial Treatments, 31
Psychotherapy, 4, 47
Risky behaviour, 33

Schizoid personality disorder, 80
Schizophrenia, 17, 23, 27
Seasonal affective disorder (SAD), 5, 60
Section 12 approved doctors, 7, 117

Self-harm, 17
Self-Help Groups, 32, 139
Seroxat, 44
Sex drive, 14
Sleep disturbance, 38
Sleep problems, 5, 35, 53
Social anxiety disorder, 6, 76
Social isolation, 16
Sodium valproate, 42
Stress, 78, 140, 145, 146
Substance use disorders, 3, 29
Suicidal tendencies, 3, 28
Suicidal thinking, 14
Suicide, 35
Symptoms, 3, 14, 24, 26, 27, 31, 85

The Court of Protection (COP), 105
The Mental Capacity Act (Northern Ireland) 2016, 110
The Mental Health (Northern Ireland) Order 1986, 131
Thought disorders, 25
Trcyclic anti-depressants, 43

Voluntary patients, 116

World Health Organisation, 13, 83

****

www.straightforwardco.co.uk

All titles, listed below, in the Straightforward Guides Series can be purchased online, using credit card or other forms of payment by going to www.straightfowardco.co.uk A discount of 25% per title is offered with online purchases.

Law

A Straightforward Guide to:

Bailiff Law-A Guide for Creditors and Debtors

Consumer Rights

Bankruptcy Insolvency and the Law

Employment Law

Private Tenants Rights

Family law

Small Claims in the County Court

Contract law

Intellectual Property and the law

Divorce and the law

Leaseholders Rights

The Process of Conveyancing

Knowing Your Rights and Using the Courts

Producing Your own Will

Housing Rights

The Bailiff the law and You

Probate and The Law

Company law

What to Expect When You Go to Court

Give me Your Money-Guide to Effective Debt Collection

General titles

Letting Property for Profit

Buying, Selling and Renting property

Buying a Home in England and France

Bookkeeping and Accounts for Small Business

Creative Writing

Freelance Writing

Writing Your own Life Story

Writing performance Poetry

Writing Romantic Fiction

Speech Writing

Teaching Your Child to Read and write

Teaching Your Child to Swim

Creating a Successful Commercial Website

The Straightforward Business Plan

The Straightforward C.V.

Successful Public Speaking

Handling Bereavement

Individual and Personal Finance

Understanding Mental Illness

The Two Minute Message

Guide to Self Defence

Go to: www.straightforwardco.co.uk